Lyman O. Littlefield

**The Martyrs**

A Sketch of the Lives and a Full Account of the Martyrdom of Joseph and

Hyrum Smit

Lyman O. Littlefield

**The Martyrs**
*A Sketch of the Lives and a Full Account of the Martyrdom of Joseph and Hyrum Smit*

ISBN/EAN: 9783337339425

Printed in Europe, USA, Canada, Australia, Japan

Cover: Foto ©Lupo / pixelio.de

More available books at **www.hansebooks.com**

# THE MARTYRS;

A SKETCH OF THE LIVES AND A FULL ACCOUNT
OF THE MARTYRDOM OF

## JOSEPH AND HYRUM SMITH,

TOGETHER WITH

A Concise Review of the Most Prominent Incidents Connected
with the Persecutions of the Saints, from the time the
Church was Organized up to the Year 1846.

BY LYMAN O. LITTLEFIELD.

JUVENILE INSTRUCTOR OFFICE,
Salt Lake City,
1882.

Entered, according to Act of Congress, in the year 1882, by George C. Lambert, in the office of the Librarian of Congress, at Washington.

# PREFACE.

SINCE the death of the Prophet and Patriarch, Joseph and Hyrum Smith, a new generation has sprang into existence. Hosts of young people are growing up in the midst of the Latter-day Saints, and still others have attained to manhood and womanhood in the Church, who never saw those noble martyrs whose lives were sacrificed in establishing the gospel upon the earth. Thousands of others have also gathered under the gospel banner from the various nations of the earth since their death. While such persons may be devoted followers of those early leaders, and may cherish a love and veneration for their memory, they are forced to depend in great part upon the verbal testimony of their parents or others who had the pleasure of a personal acquaintance, for their knowledge of the character, lives and tragic death of Joseph and Hyrum Smith. True, much has been written and published at various times in the Church upon this subject, but not in a concise and authentic shape. The facts as published are scattered through the various volumes of the *Times and Seasons, Millennial Star*, JUVENILE INSTRUCTOR and other publication, which few students have access to.

It is our intention to publish, in book form, as soon as possible, a detailed "History of Joseph Smith;" in fact, the most of the copy for it is already prepared. Believing, however, that a brief sketch of the most important scenes through which he passed, and a full account of his martyrdom, especially if written by one who was familiar with him while living, would be acceptable to our friends, we have employed Brother Littlefield to write and compile the same. Perhaps no person had better opportunities for learning the full particulars of the Carthage tragedy than he, for he was in a position at the time of the occurrence to get full and authentic information in regard to it, and took pains to do so.

Of course, the limited size of this volume will not admit of more than a brief allusion to many scenes of interest in the early history of the Church, while very many others have had to be omitted entirely. But many facts are herein narrated that have never before been published, while others have been collected from various sources and here arranged in compact form, for the use of those who may desire to learn something of the interesting subjects upon which the work treats.

That a perusal of this brief volume may tend to inspire those into whose hands it may fall with a respect for and a desire to emulate the virtues of the noble men whose lives and death it commemorates, is the desire of

THE PUBLISHER.

# CONTENTS.

### CHAPTER I.

Joseph Smith's Birth—His Family—Humble Circumstances—Joseph and Hyrum the Leading Spirits—Religious Excitement—Joseph Appeals to God—His Prayer Answered—God, the Father, and His Son, Jesus Christ, Appear and Instruct Him—Persecution which Followed the First Mention of This Vision—Visits From the Angel Moroni—Sacred Records Shown—Instructions and Predictions. Page 9.

### CHAPTER II.

The Example Set by Joseph Smith—Predictions Fulfilled in His Persecution—Proof that He Was Not a "False Prophet"—Visit and View the Sacred Records Once A Year—Obtain Possession of Them—Devices of His Enemies to Secure Them—Removal to Pennsylvania—Book of Mormon Translated and Published—Its Title an Ancient One—Church Organized—Mobbed, Tarred and Feathered—Preach to Mobbers—Child Dies—Mobs in Ohio and Missouri—Religion Their Only Offense—House Torn Down—Press Confiscated—Tarred and Feathered—Driven to Prairies and Woods—Cross the Missouri—Find Refuge. Page 17.

## CHAPTER III.

Settle in Clay, Ray, Caldwell and Daviess Counties—Far West—Hostilities Recommenced—Mob Aided by Militia—Boggs' Order to Exterminate the Saints—Haun's Mill Massacre and Other Outrages—Mob and Militia Forces Concentrated at Far West—Formed in Battle Array—Mob Outnumber the Saints Twenty-three Fold—Threatened Massacre—Hinkle's Treachery—Leading Saints Taken Prisoners—Court Martial—Sentenced to be Shot in Presence of Their Families—Doniphan's Noble Action—Prisoners Taken to Independence—Sympathy for Them—Confined in Jail, Heavily Ironed—A Prison Scene—Dignity in Chains—Prisoners Enter Liberty Jail—Given Poison and Human Flesh to Eat—The Escape.
Page 27.

## CHAPTER IV.

Saints Take Refuge in Illinois—Commerce Selected as a Gathering Place—Congress and Van Buren Appealed to for Redress of Wrongs—Van Buren's Disgraceful Reply—Nauvoo Incorporated—Hyrum Smith Made Patriarch—Joseph Smith Again Arrested—Tried Before Stephen A. Douglass—Discharged—A Prophecy—Boggs' Affidavit—Avoids Arrest—Kidnapped at Dixon—Brutal Treatment by Reynolds and Wilson—Scene at Pawpaw Grove—Friends in Nauvoo Aroused—Scour the Country in Search of Joseph—Find Him and Return to Nauvoo—An Ovation—Kidnappers Entertained as Guests—Further Efforts of Reynolds and Wilson to Cause Trouble. Page 36.

## CHAPTER V.

Review of Joseph Smith's Character—A Candidate for the Presidency of the U. S.—"Expositor" Issued—Declared a Nuisance—Abated by Order of the City Council—Efforts to take Joseph Smith to Carthage for Trial on a Charge of Riot—His Objections to Going There—Impression that He would be Murdered—The Governor Insists Upon it—Joseph Submits. Page 48.

## CHAPTER VI.

The Prophet's Last Public Speech—Start for Carthage—Remarks on Passing the Temple and Leaving 'Squire Wells—Order from the Governor to Deliver up the State Arms—Return to Nauvoo to Have the Order Complied With—Reach Carthage at Midnight—The Governor Pledges the Faith of the State for Their Protection—The Prisoners Exhibited Before the Troops—Joseph's Remarks to Officers who Visit Him. Page 59.

## CAAPTER VII.

Committed to Jail—Mob Despair of Convicting the Prisoners by Legal Process, and Determine to Effect Their Purpose by Powder and Ball—Governor Promises to Take Them to Nauvoo with Him—Sends Marshal Greene to Nauvoo to Keep Order During His Visit—Governor Ford Goes to Nauvoo, Leaving the Prisoners to their Fate—A Mob with Painted Faces Surround the Jail and Murder Joseph and Hyrum Smith and Wound John Taylor—News of the Massacre Sent to Nauvoo—Grief-stricken Community—Alarm of the Mobocrats—Arrival of the Bodies of the Martyrs.
Page 65.

## CHAPTER VIII.

Account of the Massacre by One who was Among the Mob—Probable Fate of This Informer—How He Happened to be With the Mob Party—Details of the Massacre—Reflections on the Horrible Deed—Return to His Home—A Dream—Determine to Do What He Could to Bring the Murderers to Justice—Visit to Nauvoo and Quincy—Hush-money Offered Him—He Joins the Church—Efforts to Put Him Out of the Way—Before the Grand Jury as a Witness—Nine Persons Indicted—Murderers Allowed to Go Free. Page 70.

## CHAPTER IX.

Letter From the Man Who Attempted to Cut Joseph Smith's Head Off—Corroborative of the Statement of Daniels. Page 87.

## CONTENTS.

### CHAPTER X.

Ford's Flight From Nauvoo on Hearing the Signal that the Murder Had Been Committed—Prevents the News from Being Carried to Nauvoo—His Advice to the People of Carthage to Flee—Elder Taylor's Return to Nauvoo—His Own Account of it—The Governor's Alarm—Jonas and Fellows Sent by Him to Nauvoo—Resolutions of City Council—People of Warsaw Refuse to Support the Governor—Insolent Letter From Ford. Page 90.

### CHAPTER XI.

Sidney Rigdon's Claim to Leadership—The Saints Convinced that President Young was the Man—Work on the Temple Crowded—Persecution Continued—Removal to Rocky Mountains Predicted—Suggestion From Governor Ford—A Song. Page 96.

### CHAPTER XII.

Further Outrages—Men Whipped—Others Kidnapped—Fed With Poison and Set up for Targets, but Finally Released—One-sided Court—Assassin Rule—Outrages Unbearable—Removal Westward Commenced—Nauvoo Besieged, and Remaining Saints Forcibly Driven Out.
Page 101.

### CHAPTER XIII.

Joseph Smith Arraigned on Criminal Charge Fifty Times, and Invariably Acquitted—Respect for Civil Law Enjoined by Revelation—The Saints a Loyal People.
Page 106.

### CHAPTER XIV.

Retributive Justice. Page 109.

### CHAPTER XV.

Concluding Remarks. Page 113.

# THE MARTYRS.

## CHAPTER I.

JOSEPH SMITH'S BIRTH—HIS FAMILY—HUMBLE CIRCUMSTANCES—JOSEPH AND HYRUM THE LEADING SPIRITS—RELIGIOUS EXCITEMENT — JOSEPH APPEALS TO GOD — HIS PRAYER ANSWERED — GOD THE FATHER AND HIS SON JESUS CHRIST APPEAR AND INSTRUCT HIM — PERSECUTION WHICH FOLLOWED THE FIRST MENTION OF THIS VISION — VISITS FROM THE ANGEL MORONI — SACRED RECORDS SHOWN—INSTRUCTIONS AND PREDICTIONS.

JOSEPH SMITH was born in the town of Sharon, Windsor County, Vermont, on the 23rd of December, 1805.

His brother, HYRUM SMITH, was nearly six years his senior, having been born February 9, 1800, in Tunbridge, Orange County, Vermont.

These brothers were martyred for their religion, at Carthage, Hancock County, Illinois, when in the prime of life and the bloom of manhood, but not before they had accomplished a work and left a record that will cause their names to be revered and their memories to be cherished while time shall last.

Some of the prominent incidents in the lives of these illustrious men, and the causes which led to their death, by violence, will be carefully set forth in this work and established by abundant documentary evidence, now within the reach of the author.

Joseph being the prominent actor in that which will be related, it will be proper to follow him more closely than his brother Hyrum in this narrative. Their lives were closely interwoven. No brothers ever loved each other more devotedly, or were more harmonious in their feelings, and that which relates to one may be considered almost equally applicable to the other.

Without unnecessary circumlocution, let us briefly but candidly and plainly review the public career of these remarkable men.

When Joseph was ten years old, his parents removed to Palmyra, in the State of New York. In this place, and in the neighboring town of Manchester, the family resided for about eleven years. By occupation, his father was a farmer, and, being poor, he was unable to provide his children opportunities for acquiring any other education than the common schools of the country afforded. The family was large, consisting of eleven souls, namely—Joseph Smith, Sen., Lucy Smith (the mother), Alvin, Hyrum, Joseph, Jr., Samuel Harrison, William, Don Carlos, Sophronia, Catherine and Lucy. Both parents and children were naturally moral and inclined to religion. The mother, the son Samuel Harrison, and the daughter Sophronia, were united with the Presbyterian church.

Hyrum Smith was naturally devotional, and, at a time of religious excitement which prevailed in the region where they lived in the year 1820, he also became a Presbyterian. Joseph, however, could not feel satisfied with the doctrines taught by any of the jarring religious sects of the day. He meditated much upon the subject of religion, but could derive no satisfaction from the teachings of those who professed to be the followers of Christ. Their creeds were contradictory. Every one was in opposition to the others.

Though young and unlearned, he had the good sense to understand that religious systems which clashed with each other were inconsistent with reason and sound judgment. He discarded the whole of these discordant elements, turned away from them dissatisfied, and appealed to God. For light to guide him in the right way, he began diligently to search the scriptures. In the Epistle of James (i. 5) he read: "If any of you lack wisdom, let him ask of God, that giveth to all men liberally, and upbraideth not; and it shall be given him." This passage gave him great satisfaction; it filled him with joy. There was a definite promise of help from the Almighty to all who would ask of Him.

He determined to act according to the injunction of James, and with an honest heart and pure motives, set about the delightful task.

The course immediately taken by him and the result of the same will best be understood from the following extract from "Remarkable Visions," by Apostle Orson Pratt:

"He, therefore, retired to a secret place, in a grove, but a short distance from his father's house, and knelt down and began to call upon the Lord. At first, he was severely tempted by the powers of darkness, which endeavored to overcome him, but he continued to seek for deliverance, until darkness gave way from his mind, and he was enabled to pray in fervency of the spirit, and in faith; and while thus pouring out his soul, anxiously desiring an answer from God, he saw a very bright and glorious light in the heavens above, which at first seemed to be at a considerable distance. He continued praying, while the light appeared to be gradually descending towards him; and, as it drew nearer, it increased in brightness and magnitude, so that by the time that it reached the tops of the trees, the whole wilderness, for some distance around, was illuminated in a most glorious and brilliant manner. He expected to have seen the leaves and boughs of the trees consumed, as soon as the light came in contact with them; but, perceiving that it did not produce that effect, he was encouraged with the hope of being able to endure its presence. It continued descending slowly until it rested upon the earth, and he was enveloped in the midst of it. When it first came upon him, it produced a peculiar sensation throughout his whole system; and, immediately, his mind was caught away from the natural objects with which he was surrounded, and he was enwrapped in a heavenly vision, and saw two glorious personages, who exactly resembled each other in their features or likeness. He was informed that his sins were forgiven. He was also informed upon the subjects which had for some time previously agitated his mind, namely, that all religious denominations were believing in incorrect doctrines; and, consequently, that none of them was acknowledged of God as His church and kingdom. And he was expressly commanded to go not after them: and he received a promise that the true doctrine—the fullness of the gospel—should, at some future time, be made known to him; after which, the vision withdrew, leaving his mind in a state of calmness and peace indescribable."

From the foregoing we learn how promptly the Lord answered the sincere petition of this honest-hearted boy, untutored by the learning of men, and unbiased as he was by the sophistry and vain theories which were promulgated for the doctrines of Christ.

Although visitations from heavenly beings should neither surprise nor seem unreasonable to Bible believers, (inasmuch as they were formerly common, according to scripture statements), Joseph Smith had no sooner made known the fact of his having been so favored, than he was beset by ridicule, hatred and bitter persecution from those he had formerly thought to be his friends. In his own writings upon this point, he said:

"Some few days after I had this vision, I happened to be in company with one of the Methodist preachers, who was very active in the before-mentioned religious excitement, and, conversing with him on the subject of religion. I took occasion to give him an account of the vision which I had had. I was greatly surprised at his behavior; he treated my communication not only lightly, but with great contempt, saying, it was all of the devil, that there were no such things as visions or revelations in these days; that all such things had ceased with the Apostles and that there never would be any more of them. I soon found, however, that my telling the story had excited a great deal of prejudice against me among professors of religion, and was the cause of great persecution, which continued to increase, and though I was an obscure boy, only between fourteen and fifteen years of age, and my circumstances in life such as to make a boy of no consequence in the world, yet men of high standing would take notice sufficient to excite the public mind against me, and create a hot persecution; and this was common among all the sects—all united to persecute me.

"It caused me serious reflection then, and often has since, how very strange it was that an obscure boy, of a little over fourteen years of age, and one, too, who was doomed to the necessity of obtaining a scanty maintenance by his daily labor, should be thought a character of sufficient importance to attract the attention of the great ones of the most popular sects of the day, so as to create in them a spirit of the hottest persecution and reviling. But strange or not, so it was, and was often cause of great sorrow to myself. However, it was nevertheless a fact that I had had a vision. * * * I had actually seen a light, and in the midst of that light I saw two personages, and they did in reality speak unto me, or one of them did; and though I was hated and persecuted for saying that I had seen a vision, yet it was true; and while they were persecuting me, reviling me, and speaking all manner of evil against me falsely for so saying, I was led to say in my heart, why persecute for telling the truth? I have actually seen a vision and "who am I that I can withstand God?" or why does the world think to make me deny what I have actually seen? for I had seen a vision; I knew it and I knew that God knew it, and I could not deny it, neither dare I do it; at least, I knew that by so doing I would offend God, and come under condemnation."

For three years after seeing the vision mentioned, Joseph Smith continued to endure persecution from all quarters, without receiving any other divine manifestations. On the 21st of September, 1823, however, after he had retired to rest, he besought the Lord, in fervent prayer, to send some kind messenger to commune with him and again make known His will to him. While thus praying, a bright light appeared in the room and in the midst of it was a personage whose "countenance was as lightning, yet it was of a pleasing, innocent and glorious appearance; so much so that every fear was banished from the heart, and nothing but calmness pervaded the soul." He "declared himself to be an angel of God, (Moroni) sent forth by commandment, to communicate to him that his sins were forgiven, and that his prayers were heard; and also to bring the joyful tidings, that the covenant which God made with ancient Israel concerning their posterity was at hand to be fulfilled—that the great preparatory work for the second coming of the Messiah was speedily to commence—that the time was at hand for the gospel, in its fullness, to be preached in power unto all nations, that a people might be prepared with faith and righteousness for the millennial reign of universal peace and joy."

He was further informed that he was called and chosen to be an instrument in the hands of God to bring about some of His marvelous purposes in this dispensation.

"It was also made manifest to him that the American Indians were a remnant of Israel; that when they first emigrated to America they were an enlightened people, possessing a knowledge of the true God, enjoying His favor and peculiar blessings from His hand; that the prophets and inspired writers among them, were required to keep a sacred history of the most important events transpiring among them, which history was handed down for many generations, till at length they fell into great wickedness. The greatest part of them were destroyed, and the records (by commandment of God to one of the last prophets among them,) were safely deposited to preserve them from the hands of the wicked who sought to destroy them. He was informed that these records contained many sacred revelations pertaining to the gospel of the kingdom, as well as prophecies relating to the great events of the last days; and that to fulfill His promises to the ancients, who wrote the records, and to accomplish His purposes, in the restitution of their children, etc., they were to come forth to the knowledge of the people. If faithful, he was to be the instrument who should be thus highly favored in bringing these sacred things to light; at the same time being expressly informed, that it must be done with an eye single to the glory of God, that no one could be entrusted with those sacred writings, who should endeavor to aggrandize himself, by converting sacred things to speculative purposes. After giving him many instructions concerning things past and to come, which would be foreign to our purpose to mention here, he disappeared, and the light and glory of God withdrew, leaving his mind in perfect peace, while a calmness and serenity indescribable pervaded the soul. But before morning, the vision was twice renewed, instructing him further and still further concerning the great work of God about to be performed on the earth. In the morning he went out to his work as usual, but soon the vision was renewed—the angel again appeared, and, having been informed by the previous visions of the night, concerning the place where those records were deposited, he was instructed to go immediately and view them."

Accordingly, says Joseph, "I left the field, and went to the place where the messenger had told me the plates were deposited; and owing to the distinctness of the vision which I had had concerning it, I knew the place the instant that I arrived there. Convenient to the village of Manchester, Ontario County, New York, stands a hill of considerable size, and the most elevated of any in the neighborhood. On the west side of this hill, not far from the top, under a stone of considerable size, lay the plates, deposited in a stone box. This stone was thick and rounding in the middle on the upper side, and thinner towards the edges, so that the middle part of it was visible above the ground, but the edge all round was covered with earth. Having removed the earth and obtained a lever, which I got fixed under the edge of the stone, and with a little exertion raised it up. I looked in, and there indeed did I behold the plates, the Urim and Thummim, and the breastplate, as stated by the messenger. The box in which they lay, was formed by laying stones together in some kind of cement. In the bottom of the box, were laid two stones crossways of the box, and on these stones lay the plates and the other things with them. I made an attempt to take them out, but was forbidden

## JOSEPH'S FIRST VISIT TO THE HILL CUMORAH. 15

by the messenger, and was again informed that the time for bringing them forth had not yet arrived, neither would, until four years from that time; but he told me that I should come to that place precisely in one year from that time, and that he would there meet with me, and that I should continue to do so until the time should come for obtaining the plates."

As Joseph stood by the sacred deposit "gazing and admiring, the angel said. 'Look!' And as he thus spake, he beheld the Prince of Darkness, surrounded by his innumerable train of associates. All this passed before him, and the heavenly messenger said, 'All this is shown, the good and the evil, the holy and impure, the glory of God, and the power of darkness, that you may know hereafter the two powers, and never be influenced or overcome by the wicked one. Behold, whatsoever enticeth and leadeth to good and to do good is of God, and whatsoever doth not is of that wicked one. It is he that filleth the hearts of men with evil, to walk in darkness and blaspheme God; and you may learn from henceforth that his ways are to destruction, but the way of holiness is peace and rest. You cannot, at this time, obtain this record, for the commandment of God is strict, and if ever these sacred things are obtained, they must be by prayer and faithfulness in obeying the Lord.'"

Many other principles were revealed to Joseph by the angel, who then made the following prophetic declarations:

"I give unto you another sign, and when it comes to pass, then know that the Lord is God, and that He will fulfill His purposes, and that the knowledge which this record contains will go to every nation, and kindred, and tongue, and people under the whole heaven. This is the sign: when these things begin to be known, that is, when it is known that the Lord has shown you these things, the workers of iniquity will seek your overthrow. They will circulate falsehoods to destroy your reputation, and also will seek to take your life; but remember this, if you are faithful and shall hereafter continue to keep the commandments of the Lord, you shall be preserved to bring these things forth; for in due time He will give you a commandment to come and take them. When they are interpreted, the Lord will give the holy priesthood to some, and they shall begin to proclaim this gospel and baptize by water, and after that they shall have power to give the Holy Ghost by the laying on of their hands. Then will persecution rage more and more; for the iniquities of men shall be revealed, and those who are not built upon the Rock will seek to overthrow the church; but it will increase the more opposed, and spread farther and farther, increasing in knowledge till they shall be sanctified, and receive an inheritance where the glory of God will rest upon them; and when this takes place, and all things are prepared, the ten tribes of Israel will be revealed in the north country, whither they have been for a long season; and when this is fulfilled will be brought to pass that saying of the prophet,—'And the Redeemer shall come to Zion, and unto them that turn from trangression in Jacob, saith the Lord.' But notwithstanding the workers of iniquity shall seek your destruction, the arm of the Lord will be extended, and you will be borne off conqueror if you keep all His commandments. Your name shall be known among the nations, for the work which the Lord will perform by your hands shall cause the righteous to rejoice and the wicked to rage; with the one it shall be had in honor, and with the other in reproach; yet, with these it shall be a terror, because of the great and marvelous work which shall follow the coming forth of this fullness of the gospel. Now, go thy way, remembering what the Lord hath done for thee, and be diligent in keeping His commandments, and He will deliver thee from temptations and all the arts and devices of the wicked one. Forget not to pray, that thy mind may become strong, that when He shall manifest unto thee thou mayest have power to escape the evil and obtain these precious things."

After this vision, Joseph, in consequence of the poor circumstances of his father, left home and obtained employment from a Mr. Josiah Stoal, of Chenango County, New York. While employed by this gentleman, he became acquainted with Miss Emma Hale, daughter of Isaac Hale. This acquaintance resulted in the marriage of the two on the 27th of January, 1827. Miss Hale's parents were, at first, much opposed to the match, on account of the strong prejudice against Joseph, resulting from his having seen a vision; but they finally became reconciled.

## CHAPTER II.

THE EXAMPLE SET BY JOSEPH SMITH — PREDICTIONS FULFILLED IN HIS PERSECUTION—PROOF THAT HE WAS NOT A "FALSE PROPHET" — VISIT AND VIEW THE SACRED RECORDS ONCE A YEAR—OBTAIN POSSESSION OF THEM— DEVICES OF HIS ENEMIES TO SECURE THEM — REMOVAL TO PENNSYLVANIA — BOOK OF MORMON TRANSLATED AND PUBLISHED — ITS TITLE AN ANCIENT ONE—CHURCH ORGANIZED — MOBBED, TARRED AND FEATHERED — PREACH TO MOBBERS—CHILD DIES—MOBS IN OHIO AND MISSOURI—RELIGION THEIR ONLY OFFENSE—HOUSE TORN DOWN — PRESS CONFISCATED—TARRED AND FEATHERED —DRIVEN TO PRAIRIES AND WOODS — CROSS THE MISSOURI—FIND REFUGE.

THE reader will bear in mind that all the manifestations and revelations mentioned in the foregoing quotations, were given to Joseph from early in the spring of 1820, up to the 21st of September, 1823.

These precious blessings were bestowed upon him through the channel which the Lord has ordained by which a knowledge of Himself, together with the doctrines of salvation, are to flow to the children of men. These blessings were given in answer to the prayer of faith, rendered to Him from a sincere and honest heart. And these things took place at a time when "darkness covered the earth and gross darkness the minds of the people. (*Isaiah* xxix. 13-14.) "Wherefore the Lord said, Forasmuch as this people draw near me with their mouth, and with their lips do honor me, but have removed their heart far from me, and their fear toward me is taught by the precepts of men: therefore, behold, I will proceed to do a marvelous work among this people, even a marvelous work and a wonder: for the wisdom of their wise men shall perish, and the understanding of their prudent shall be hid."

To be sure, people prayed in those days; they offered long prayers, to be seen and heard of men, in public places, (as many do now), that they might get praise. But here was a youth who was honest-hearted. Reared to follow his father's plow, he imbibed inspirations of humility from the rural walks of life — amidst fields and woods, the hills and and waving grain, and, like David of old, among the lowing herds. His mind was untainted by the conflict of opinions that jarred the sects and turned their feet from the old paths where apostles and prophets were wont to tread. He looked in vain to the existing creeds. In his honest soul there was a void they could not fill; a longing for certainties they could not produce. Turning from them all, retreating from the gaze of men, he sought seclusion in the silent woods, where no eyes could behold and no ears hear him but those of God and His angels. "He that asketh in secret shall be rewarded openly," is a promise made by the Savior Himself, agreeing with that of James, already quoted; and, by acting in accordance with these, Joseph Smith proved himself worthy of, and actually did receive, the promised blessing.

Yet when he told what he had seen and heard, he was mocked, abused, and shunned by the wicked; and professors of religion declared it could not be true that he had been favored with a vision; that he had not heard the voices of the Father and the Son; that he had not seen an holy angel and listened to inspired words from his lips; for, said they, these things all ceased with the ancients; they are all done away, and God will never more appear to men in the flesh or send angels to reveal His will.

It is ardently hoped that the rising generation, the young especially among the Latter-day Saints, will use this great key to which reference is here made and follow the example of the prophet Joseph in his boyhood, that none of them may longer say they believe the gospel is true because father and mother say so; but that they may learn from God, by the manifestations of His Spirit to them, that the gospel is true; that God lives and His kingdom is being established upon the earth to stand forever.

This knowledge is within their reach. Ask and receive; inquire and you will not be turned away empty; but you can *know* of these things for "yourselves and not for another." It is, in part, for the benefit of the youth, the thousands who have been born since the martyrdom of Joseph and Hyrum Smith, as well as the multitudes of people who have since come from the nations of the earth and the islands of the sea, that the writer has undertaken to collate and print some of the leading facts connected with the rise of this Church and the martyrdom of these first and leading champions of the work of God upon the earth.

But the oldest living members of the Church; those who have stood side by side with these noble martyrs; those who were with them in prison; those who offered their lives to save that of the Prophet, and were the guards and protectors of his person; those who have passed through mobs and seen the blood of the innocent shed without provocation; those who have been deprived of liberty and driven into exile, and whose forms are bent with exposure and whose heads are white with the frosts of time—they, too, may derive some consolation by perusing this brief narrative of past incidents in which they were honored to take a part.

Special attention should be given to the latter portion of the angel's message, which foretold the persecutions in store for Joseph, and not for him alone, but for all those who should thereafter receive the Priesthood and take a part in the ministry. Throughout the whole of Joseph Smith's life, from that time up to his tragic death, as will be seen from the incidents herein narrated, the words of the angel were literally fulfilled, and they have, also, up to the present day, been proved true in the case of those who accepted the testimony of Joseph and obeyed the gospel he taught. These things were thus declared in the very beginning, and marked out as being among the characteristic features of the people of God, until the Prince of Darkness shall be overthrown.

Thus was Joseph Smith given to understand, in the very commencemet of his public career, what he might expect as a consequence of his obedience to the requirements of the Almighty; and had he not been a noble spirit and inspired for the work, he must certainly have shrunk from the task. The fact of his making known these predictions of the angel, and thus warning his followers of what they must undergo, is a strong proof that he was not the "false prophet" that many have declared him to be, and that he had no ulterior motives in asking people to accept the doctrines he taught. A false prophet, establishing a delusion, would have offered a more tempting picture than this to those he wished to ensnare.

Once in each year, after the interview with the angel, before referred to, in 1823, Joseph repaired to the hill where the plates were still deposited, where he, each time, met with this same heavenly messenger and received much further instruction, until the time had fully arrived when the plates were to be delivered into his hands, which took place on the 22nd of September, 1827. And so true were the words of the angel as to the persecutions that were to befall Joseph, when he should come in possession of these sacred records, that while he was returning home, with them in his possession, he was waylaid by two men who had secreted themselves purposely to rob him. He was struck with a club; but finally succeeded in eluding them and reached his father's house in safety.

False rumors and misrepresentations, as to his character, were put in circulation. "The house was frequently beset by mobs and evil designing persons. Several times he was shot at and very narrowly escaped. Every device was used to get the plates away from him. And being continually in danger of his life from a gang of abandoned wretches, he at length concluded to leave the place and go to Pennsylvania; and accordingly packed up his goods, putting the plates in a barrel of beans, and proceeded upon his journey. He had not gone far before he was overtaken by an officer with a search-warrant, who flattered himself with the idea that he should surely obtain the plates. After searching very diligently, he was sadly disappointed at not finding them. Joseph drove on, but before he got to his journey's end he was again overtaken by an officer on the same business, and after ransacking the wagon very carefully, he went his way as much chagrinned as the first, at not being able to discover the object of his research. Without any further molestation he pursued his journey until he came into the northern part of Pennsylvania, near the Susquehannah river, in which part his father-in-law resided."

As soon as he provided himself with a home, he began the translation of the plates, by the gift and power of God, through the means of the Urim and Thummim. This he continued, having for his scribe, most of the time, Oliver Cowdery, until the records upon the plates were all translated with the exception of some which were sealed, and which the angel informed him were not then to be translated. The portion translated was finally printed in the fore part of the year 1830, the means to defray the expense of the same being furnished by Martin Harris.

In relation to the title of the book, Joseph says, in his history:

"I wish to mention here, that the title page of the Book of Mormon is a literal translation, taken from the very last leaf, on the left hand side of the collection or book of plates, which contained the record which has been translated, the language of the whole running the same as all Hebrew writing in general; and that said title page is not by any means a modern composition, either of mine or any other man's who has lived or does live in this generation. Therefore, in order to correct an error which generally exists concerning it, I give below that part of the title page of the English version of the Book of Mormon which is a genuine and literal translation of the title page of the original book of Mormon, as recorded on the plates —

### THE BOOK OF MORMON.

*An account written by the hand of Mormon, upon Plates, taken from the Plates of Nephi.*"

In the meantime the Church of Jesus Christ of Latter-day Saints had been organized. This organization was the result of revelations to Joseph Smith, and occurred at the house of Peter Whitmer, Sen., in Fayette, Seneca County, State of New York, on the sixth day of April, A. D., eighteen hundred and thirty. Joseph had also received many visits from heavenly beings conferring keys upon him which they had held in former dispensations—the keys of the Aaronic and Melchisedek Priesthoods, etc.

The principal theme dwelt upon in this little volume, is, in some respects, an unpleasant one. It is not agreeable to dwell upon topics which rend the heart and shock sensibility; but when deeds of violence have been committed and the innocent plunged into conditions of unmerited suffering, it is but the performance of duty to vindicate the injured. When the honest and meek in heart are maligned and their best and noblest motives construed for evil, it is but the work of justice that the pen should wield its potent influence in their defense. When the high-minded are sought to be debased, and the patriotic and loyal have their truest acts of allegiance given the coloring of treason, by unprincipled religious partizans, it should be the privilege of any who choose, to champion their just cause. It is painful to reflect that deeds partaking of barbaric cruelty, like the ones still to be referred to, have really transpired in our beloved America, the land of boasted political liberty and freedom of conscience.

The rage, malice and wicked feeling that existed in the hearts of the ungodly against Joseph and Hyrum Smith were not just fanned into a blaze during the last few months of their citizenship in Illinois. As already shown, this cruel and unrelenting spirit of mobocracy was inaugurated from the very day and hour that Joseph was charged with the Divine trust and became the chosen mouthpiece of God to man. And, not Joseph and Hyrum Smith only, but, after the Church was organized and the Priesthood was conferred upon others and they began to preach the gospel and to baptize by immersion in water, and they held the power to confer the Holy Ghost by the laying on of hands, then, as the angel foretold, did "persecution rage more and more." All who took a part in the ministry in those early times, and those who have done so from that day to the present, have had to contend with the powers and machinations of the Prince of Darkness.

An account of the mobbing which took place (March 25th, 1832,) at Hiram, where Joseph lived, at the time, with "Father Johnson," is thus related by Joseph:

"On the 25th of March, the twins before mentioned, which had been sick of the measles for some time, caused us to be broken of our rest in taking care of them, especially my wife. In the evening I told her she had better retire to rest with one of the children, and I would watch with the sickest child. In the night she told me I had better lay down on the trundle bed, and I did so, and was soon after awoke by her screaming *murder!* when I found myself going out of the door, in the hands of about a dozen men; some of whose hands were in my hair, and some hold of my shirt, drawers and limbs. The foot of the trundle bed was towards the door, leaving only room enough for the door to swing. My wife heard a gentle tapping on the windows, which she then took no particular notice of, (but which was unquestionably designed for ascertaining whether we were all asleep,) and soon after the mob burst open the door and surrounded the bed in an instant, and, as I said, the first I knew I was going out of the door in the hands of an infuriated mob. I made a desperate struggle, as I was forced out, to extricate myself, but only cleared one leg, with which I made a pass at one man, and he fell on the door steps. I was immediately confined again; and they swore by God, they would kill me if I did not be still, which quieted me. As they passed around the house with me, the fellow that I kicked came to me and thrust his hand into my face, all covered with blood, (for I hit him on the nose,) and with an exulting horse laugh, muttered; 'ge, gee, *G—d damn ye, I'll fix ye.*

"Then they seized me by the throat, and held on till I lost my breath. After I came to, as they passed along with me, about thirty rods from the house, I saw Elder Rigdon stretched out on the ground, whither they had dragged him by the heels. I supposed he was dead.

"I began to plead with them, saying, 'you will have mercy, and spare my life, I hope.' To which they replied, '*G—d damn ye,* call on yer *God* for help, we'll show ye no mercy;' and the people began to show themselves in every direction; one coming from the orchard had a plank, and I expected they would kill me, and carry me off on the plank. They then turned to the right, and went on about thirty rods farther, about sixty rods from the house, and thirty from where I saw Elder Rigdon, into the meadow, where they stopped, and one said, 'Simonds, Simonds' (meaning, I supposed, Simonds Rider,) 'pull up his drawers, pull up his drawers, he will take cold.' Another replied: '*aint ye going to kill 'im? aint ye going to kill 'im?*' when a group of mobbers collected a little way off, and said: 'Simonds, Simonds, come here;' and Simonds charged those who had hold of me to keep me from touching the ground, (as they had done all the time) lest I should get a spring upon them. They went and held a council, and as I could occasionally overhear a word, I supposed it was to know whether it was best to kill me. They returned, after a while, when I learned that they had concluded not to kill me, but pound and scratch me well, tear off my shirt and drawers, and leave me naked; one cried, 'Simonds, Simonds, *where's the tar* bucket?' 'I don't know,' answered one, 'where 'tis; Eli's left it.' They ran back and fetched the bucket of tar, when one exclaimed, 'G—d damn it, let us tar up his mouth;' and they tried to force the tar-paddle into my mouth; I twisted my head around, so that they could not; and they cried out, 'G—d damn ye, hold up yer head, and let us give ye some tar.' They then tried to force a vial into my mouth, and broke it in my teeth. All my clothes were torn off me except my shirt collar; and one man fell on me and scratched my body with his nails like a mad cat, and then muttered out: 'G—d damn ye, that's the way the Holy Ghost falls on folks.'

"They then left me, and I attempted to arise, but fell again; I pulled the tar away from my lips, etc., so that I could breathe more freely, and after awhile I began to recover, and raised myself up, when I saw two lights. I made my way towards one of them, and found it was Father Johnson's. When I had come to the door, I was naked, and the tar made me look as though I had been covered with blood, and when my wife saw me she thought I was all mashed to pieces, and fainted. During the affray abroad, the sisters of the neighborhood had collected at my room. I called for a blanket; they threw me one and shut the door; I wrapped it around me and went in."

In this inhuman onslaught, Sidney Rigdon was dragged by his heels over the frozen ground until his head was badly lascerated, which rendered him delirious for several days. "Father Johnson" was also roughly handled. Joseph's friends spent the remainder of the night in removing the tar and washing and cleansing his body, so that he could be clothed again. The next day was Sunday, and, true to his mission, and agreeably with his determined purpose to do the will of heaven, he went to meeting, with his "flesh all scarified and defaced," and preached to a congregation, among whom were the identical mobbers who had thus invaded his home, dragged him from his imploring wife and sick children, and abused him in a manner disgraceful even to the character of savages.

Owing to the exposure to which the sick children were subjected through this sudden and cruel demonstration, one of them received a severe cold and died soon afterwards.

The mobbers were mostly, if not entirely, professors of religion. Simonds Rider, the leader of the mob, was a Campbellite preacher. Not satisfied with the cruelties inflicted, they kept up their aggressive demonstrations around "Father Johnson's" for some time afterwards.

The spirit of mobocracy also prevailed, at that time, in Kirtland, (Ohio,) and, more or less, all through that region of country the Saints were much opposed and persecuted. And it was not confined to that locality.

In Missouri, at Independence, Jackson County, where a colony or settlement of some twelve or fifteen hundred Latter-day Saints were located, great troubles and perplexities existed.

It is regretted that the limits of these pages will not admit of giving a more lengthy account of these difficulties. But let us glance at a few of their leading features.

The Saints in Jackson County were generally poor as to this world's goods; yet, by their industry, they had provided themselves generally with homes and purchased extensive tracts of land. A printing press had been established and a paper was printed monthly, entitled *The Evening and Morning Star*, edited by W. W. Phelps. Sidney A. Gilbert was conducting quite a thriving mercantile business, and several mechanical industries engaged the attention of their enterprising artizans; but agriculture was their most common pursuit.

Their religion taught them to respect the laws of the State, which they studiously observed; but their union and conscientious convictions of the true and living God, stood out in plain contradistinction to the conflicting sentiments and confused ideas of the religionists of that region, and herein was the *bona fide* cause of their offending. For this their neighbors should not have felt agrieved, as the religion taught by our people was the true religion of the Bible, which was everywhere held up as the foundation for Christian belief. Faith in God and in His Son Jesus Christ, repentance and baptism for the remission of sins, and the laying on of hands for the reception of the Holy Ghost, by those holding the Priesthood, were among the leading doctrines. But they said the Saints were presumptuous and believed in prophets, in apostles, in gifts of healing, in speaking in unknown tongues, in dreams and visions, in the ministration of angels, and in revelations from God to the children of men. The Saints plead guilty to all these charges, and announced many glorious things besides as being among their belief, and which were in accordance with scriptural evidence and the prophetic declarations of the long list of ancient prophets who left their-testimonies upon the sacred pages of holy writ. But that they were peace-breakers, disloyal, opposed to the laws of the State and Constitution of the United States, they plainly denied.

This hatred against the Jackson County Saints eventuated in the most bitter hostility:

"On the 20th of July, 1833, a mob collected [at Independence] and demanded the discontinuance of the printing in Jackson County—the closing of the store—and the cessation of all mechanical labors. The brethren refused compliance, and the consequence was, that the house of W. W. Phelps, which contained the printing establishment, was thrown down, the materials taken possession of by the mob, many papers destroyed, and the family and furniture thrown out of doors."

The mob then proceeded to violence towards Edward Partridge, the Bishop of the Church. They stripped him of his hat, coat and vest, and daubed him with tar from head to foot. Charles Allen was treated in the same ruthless manner, all because they would not agree to leave the country, or deny "Mormonism."

On the morning of the 23rd of July; on the nights of the 31st of October and the 1st of November, and also on the 4th of November, mobbing parties gathered in the different settlements of the brethren about the Blue river, and Independence, and committed many acts of barbarism, really shocking to humanity. Houses were demolished; the Saints were shot at and beaten with guns, sticks, etc., and women and children fled for their lives to the prairies and woods. On the nights of November 5th and 6th, women and children continued to flee before the relentless mob.

On the 7th of November, 1833, the banks of the Missouri river began to be thronged with homeless outcasts—the Saints of the living God—and the ferrymen were using their best energies to convey them to the Clay County shore, where they found temporary refuge from their infuriated assailants.

## CHAPTER III.

SETTLE IN CLAY, RAY CALDWELL AND DAVIES COUNTIES—FAR WEST—HOSTILITIES RECOMMENCED—MOB AIDED BY MILITIA—BOGGS' ORDER TO EXTERMINATE THE SAINTS—HAUN'S MILL MASSACRE AND OTHER OUTRAGES—MOB AND MILITIA FORCES CONCENTRATED AT FAR WEST—FORMED IN BATTLE ARRAY—MOB OUTNUMBER SAINTS TWENTY-THREE FOLD—THREATENED MASSACRE—HINKLE'S TREACHERY—LEADING SAINTS TAKEN PRISONERS—COURT MARTIAL—SENTENCED TO BE SHOT IN PRESENCE OF THEIR FAMILIES—DONIPHAN'S NOBLE ACTION—PRISONERS TAKEN TO INDEPENDENCE—SYMPATHY FOR THEM—CONFINED IN JAIL, HEAVILY IRONED—A PRISON SCENE—DIGNITY IN CHAINS—PRISONERS ENTER LIBERTY JAIL—GIVEN POISON AND HUMAN FLESH TO EAT—THE ESCAPE.

FOR some time after the expulsion of the Saints from Jackson County, they were permitted to dwell in comparative peace in Clay and Ray Counties. Finally they commenced to remove into the Counties of Caldwell and Davis, which were newly organized, and where much of the land was still the property of the government, to which titles could be secured under the laws of pre-emption. In Caldwell they surveyed off and built up the well known city of Far West.

This place is located about fifty miles east of the Missouri River, and sixty miles from Independence, upon a high rolling prairie. Its elevation commands a convenient view for miles around. The face of the country is undulating, and interspersed with lines of timber that skirt the margins of several small but living streams. At no very great distance, heavier bodies of timber break the monotony of the prairie scene. Everything conspires to make the situation delightful. The soil is a dark loam, rich and productive. It soon became a place of considerable business. Several dry-goods stores and a variety of mechanical pursuits were conducted. Comfortable dwellings were erected and the ground excavated for the foundation of a temple.

As a result of their habitual industry and thrift, farms were opened, grain was abundantly raised, and the Saints found themselves once more in the enjoyment of all necessary temporal comforts.

Soon their prosperity, coupled with union, excited the envy and jealousy of the citizens of the adjacent Counties, and the old Jackson County mob spirit began to be rekindled in their bosoms. In Carroll and Saline Counties, in particular, public meetings were held by the citizens to consider what could be done with the "Mormons." They went so far as to pass resolutions declaring their intentions to do all in their power to "drive the citizens belonging to the Church from their Counties, and, if possible, from the State."

As a kind of auxiliary force, to act in sympathy with these treasonable movements, a company of one thousand men were marched into Davies County. and served thirty days, under the command of Major General Atchison and Brigader Generals Parks and Doniphan. At least, this force did not seem to use its energies to guard the liberties and rights of the people, except in the immediate vicinity of their encampment. as the mob forces were allowed to roam at will and burn and plunder without restraint.

Soon after, the notorious mobocrat, Lilburn W. Boggs—then governor of the State—issued his cruel and unjustifiable exterminating order, and called out a force of ten thousand men, under the command of General Clark, to enforce its execution. The express orders were to exterminate the "Mormons," or drive them from the State.

In addition to Clark's force, another one of three or four thousand strong, under Major General D. Lucas and Brigadier General Moses Wilson, made up chiefly of the old Jackson County mobocrats, preceded the arrival of General Clark, to the city of Far West.

In the meantime, the citizens of Caldwell and Davis had not been idle. Everything in their power had been done to preserve their liberties and the lives of their wives and children. Many of the outer settlements were vacated by them and their corn fields were trodden down by the horses of these ruthless brigands. Numbers of the inhabitants fled to Far West for protection. The notorious Cornelius Gillum, with a band of desperadoes, painted as Indian warriors, had made raids through the settlements, plundering and committing murders. Another company from Carroll County had murdered some eighteen or twenty men, women and children at Haun's Mill.

These forces swelled the ranks of Lucas, at Goose Creek, as that General first began to menace Far West.

The combined forces of Clark, Lucas, Gillum, etc., numbered some sixteen thousand, perhaps more.

The force of militia at Far West did not number more than about six or seven hundred.

Not much more than one mile separated the two forces.

What was to be done? This was a momentous question, and one which must be decided without delay.

A white flag was sent out by each party. They met between the armies. The message from the assailants was: "We want three persons out of the city before we massacre the rest."

Our people on learning that this formidable force were acting by the orders of the governor, came to the conclusion not to oppose any properly authorized force, but to submit to their demands, however unjust they might be.

Not to be tedious, it need only be said here that the result was, that, by the treachery of Colonel George M. Hinkle. Messrs. Joseph Smith, Sidney Rigdon. Hyrum Smith, Lyman Wight, George Robinson and Parley P. Pratt were delivered up to the enemy, under the "assurance that as soon as peaceable arrangements could be entered into," they should be released.

But brief allusions have herein been made to the causes which led to the Missouri troubles and the final surrender of these men. Nor have a hundredth part of the cruelties inflicted upon an innocent people for their religion been stated. By referring to the "History of Joseph Smith" and the "Autobiography of Parley P. Pratt," the reader can find full and detailed accounts of these things. Neither is there space in this volume to record fully the history of their cruel treatment while held as prisoners.

The very first night they were taken into custody a council of the officers, or court martial, sentenced them to be shot, notwithstanding Lucas' assurance of protection and liberty as soon as peaceable arrangements could be entered into. This was to take place the following morning at eight o'clock, in the public square at Far West. It was, however, prevented by Brigadier General Doniphan, who was in the council, and threatened to withdraw his command if they did not retract. Said he: "It is cold blooded murder, and I wash my hands of it."

They were allowed to take a hurried leave of their heart-broken families and were forced away by their relentless captors to Independence, Jackson County, where they "were paraded in martial triumph through the principal streets, the bugles sounding a blast of triumphant joy."

It is strange that in that hot-bed of mobocracy, where in 1832-3, the people raged and imagined vain things; in that County where the abodes of peace and industry were torn down and committed to the devouring element; where women and children, dismayed, fled to the woods and cheerless prairies for safety, while frosts and piercing winds chilled their scantily-clad forms; where conscientious worshipers were driven from the sacred altars where they offered their devotions; where American citizens were driven from their lands and denied the sacred rights of citizenship; yes, it is indeed strange, that in such a locality, such a people could be touched with the sanctifying emotions of sympathy and kindness towards the noble prisoners in their midst—and these prisoners the earthly head of that religion which they spurned and the devotees of which they had so relentlessly driven from their borders. Yet their feelings were touched and their hearts softened, as may be seen by the following from the writings of Parley P. Pratt, a fellow prisoner with the Prophet:

"A vacant house was prepared for our reception, into which we were ushered through the crowd of spectators which thronged every avenue.

"The troops were then disbanded. In the meantime we were kept under a small guard, and were treated with some degree of humanity, while hundreds flocked to see us day after day. We spent most of our time in preaching and conversation, explanatory of our doctrines and practice. Much prejudice was removed, and the feelings of the populace began to be in our favor, notwithstanding their former wickedness and hatred. In a day or two we were at liberty to walk the streets without a guard. We were finally removed from our house of confinement to a hotel, where we boarded at the public table, and lodged on the floor, with a block of wood for a pillow. We no longer had any guard; we went out and came in when we pleased—a certain keeper being appointed merely to watch over us, and look to or wants.

"With him we walked out of town to the westward, and visited the desolate lands of the Saints, and the place which, seven years before, we had dedicated for the building of a Temple. This was a beautiful rise of ground, about half a mile west of Independence centre. When we saw it last it was a noble forest, but our enemies had since robbed it of every vestige of timber, and it now lay desolate, or clothed with grass and weeds.

"O, how many feelings did this spot awaken in our bosoms! Here we had often bowed the knee in prayer, in bygone years. Here we had assembled with hundreds of happy Saints in the solemn meeting, and offered our songs, and sacraments, and orisons. But now all was solemn and lonely desolation. Not a vestige remained to mark the spot where stood our former dwellings. They had long since been consumed by fire, or removed and converted to the uses of our enemies.

"While at Independence, we were once or twice invited to dine with General Wilson and some others, which we did.

"While thus sojourning as prisoners at large, I arose one morning when it was very snowy, and passed silently and unmolested out of the hotel, and, as no one seemed to notice me, or call me in question, I thought I would try an experiment. I passed on eastward through the town ; no one noticed me. I then took into the fields, still unobserved. After traveling a mile I entered a forest: all was gloomy silence, none were near, the heavens were darkened and obscured by falling snow, my track was covered behind me, and I was free. I knew the way to the States eastward very well, and there seemed nothing to prevent my pursuing my way thither; thoughts of freedom beat high in my bosom ; wife, children, home, freedom, peace, and a land of law and order, all arose in my mind: I could go to other States, send for my family, make me a home, and be happy.

"On the other hand. I was a prisoner in a State where all law was at an end. I was liable to be shot down at any time without judge or jury. I was liable to be tried for my life by murderous assassins, who had already broken every oath of office, and trampled on every principle of honor or even humanity. Hands already dripping with the blood of aged sires, and of helpless women and children, were reaching out for my destruction. The battle of Crooked River had already been construed into *murder* on the part of the brave patriots who there defended their lives and rescued their fellow citizens from kidnappers and land pirates, while the pirates themselves had been converted into loyal militia.

"To go forward was freedom, to go backward was to be sent to General Clark, and be accused of the highest crimes, with murderers for judge, jury, and executioners.

"'Go free!' whispered the tempter.

"'No!' said I, 'never, while Joseph and his fellows are in the power of the enemy. What a storm of trouble, or even of death, it might subject them to.'

"I turned on my heel, retraced my steps, and entered the hotel ere they had missed me. As I shook the snow off my clothes, the keeper and also brother Joseph inquired where I had been. I replied, just out for a little exercise. A walk for pleasure in such a storm gave rise to some pleasantries on their part, and there the matter ended.

"There was one thing which buoyed up our spirits continually during our captivity: it was the remembrance of the word of the Lord to brother Joseph, saying that our lives should all be given us during this captivity, and not one of them should be lost. I thought of this while in the wilderness vacillating whether to go or stay, and the thought struck me: '*He that will seek to save his life shall lose it; but he that will lose his life for my sake shall find it again, even life eternal.*' I could now make sure of my part in the first resurrection, as I had so intensely desired when about eleven years old. But O, the path of life! How was it beset with trials!

"At length, after repeated demands, we were sent to General Clark, at Richmond, Ray County. Generals Lucas and Wilson had tried in vain for some days to get a guard to accompany us. None would volunteer, and when drafted they would not obey orders; for, in truth, they wished us to go at liberty. At last a colonel and two or three officers started with us, with their swords and pistols, which were intended more to protect us than to keep us from escaping. On this journey some of us rode in carriages and some on horseback. Sometimes we were sixty or eighty rods in front or rear of our guards, who were drinking hard out of bottles which they carried in their pockets.

"At night, having crossed the Missouri River, we put up at a private house. Here our guards all got drunk, and went to bed and to sleep, leaving us their pistols to defend ourselves in case of any attack from without, as we were in a very hostile neighborhood."

Thus we see how the Lord can work upon the hearts of the children of men, and soften their feelings toward His chosen servants and people, when they are humble and ask in faith.
The prisoners were here received by Col. Sterling Price and accompanying posse, who conveyed them to Richmond, Ray County, where they underwent an *ex parte* examination before Judge Austin A. King, which continued from the 11th to the 28th of November, and resulted in the committal of Joseph Smith, Hyrum Smith, Sidney Rigdon, Lyman Wight, Caleb Baldwin and Alexander McRae to the jail of Clay County on the charge of treason; and Morris Phelps, Lyman Gibbs, Darwin Chase, Norman Shearer, and Parley P. Pratt, were committed to the jail of Richmond, Ray County, for the alleged crime of murder, said to have been committed in the act of dispersing the bandit, Bogart, and his gang.

The following eloquent extract is also taken from the writings of Apostle P. P. Pratt. It describes a scene that took place in the prison at Richmond, during their confinement there, and illustrates one of the noble and fearless traits so often exhibited in Joseph's character, when aroused with feelings of righteous indignation:

"In one of those tedious nights, we had lain as if in sleep till the hour of midnight had passed, and our ears and hearts had been pained, while we had listened for hours to the obscene jests, the horrid oaths, the dreadful blasphemies and filthy language of our guards, Colonel Price at their head, as they recounted to each other their deeds of rapine, murder, robbery, etc., which they had committed among the 'Mormons,' while at Far West and vicinity. They even boasted of defiling by force, wives, daughters, and virgins, and of shooting or dashing out the brains of men, women, and children.

"I had listened till I became so disgusted, shocked, horrified, and so filled with the spirit of indignant justice, that I could scarcely refrain from rising upon my feet and rebuking the guards; but had said nothing to Joseph, or any one else, although I lay next to him, and knew he was awake. On a sudden he arose to his feet, and spoke in a voice of thunder, or as the roaring lion, uttering, as near as I can recollect the following words:

"'*SILENCE, ye fiends of the infernal pit. In the name of Jesus Christ I rebuke you, and command you to be still; I will not live another minute and hear such language. Cease such talk, or you or I die* THIS INSTANT!'

"He ceased to speak. He stood erect in terrible majesty. Chained, and without a weapon; calm, unruffled, and dignified as an angel, he looked upon the quailing guards, whose weapons were lowered or dropped to the ground; whose knees smote together, and who, shrinking into a corner, or crouching at his feet, begged his pardon, and remained quiet till a change of guards.

"I have seen the ministers of justice, clothed in magisterial robes, and criminals arraigned before them, while life was suspended on a breath, in the courts of England; I have witnessed a congress in solemn session to give laws to nations; I have tried to conceive of kings, of royal courts, of thrones and crowns, and of emperors assembled to decide the fate of kingdoms; but dignity and majesty have I seen but *once*, as it stood in chains, at midnight, in a dungeon, in an obscure village of Missouri."

The prisoners committed to the Clay County jail had irons placed upon them. They were then ordered into a large wagon and driven to Liberty, Clay County, and thrust into prison.

The entrance of these noble prisoners into the town of Liberty was witnessed by the writer. The wagon that contained them had a large, high box, so that very little could be seen of the occupants below their heads and shoulders. They passed through the principal streets. Everybody, ladies and gentlemen, freemen and slaves, whites, blacks and mulattoes, all jostled together in an excitement to see the "Mormon Prophet." They looked and gazed, and all expressed the same opinion: "Well, they're fine looking men if they are Mormons." "The Prophet looks like a gentleman."

After reaching the jail, the prisoners left the wagon, and, one by one, ascended the steps to a landing or platform in front of the entrance. Their steps were firm, and their forms erect, notwithstanding irons had been put upon them when they took the wagon at Richmond. Joseph was the last of them who entered the jail, and, before doing so, he turned around and surveyed the large crowd that had collected. He wore a suit of black, and a cloak of dark color hung on his arm. He uncovered his head, and, with stately dignity in his movement, as his tall, manly form turned to enter the prison, said. "Good afternoon, gentlemen," and the prison door was closed behind him.

This movement made the spectators very angry. They said Joseph was defiant and did it for bravado. They declared he meant, by the expression "good afternoon," to make his escape that night. Joseph, being an eastern man, expressed himself according to eastern custom. A western man might have said, "good evening." And, for this slight discrepancy, a few wished him immediately brought out, that they might treat him with violence. The jailor prevented this; and, after the crowd had delivered many wicked oaths and gesticulated their vengeance, they filed away from the jail, and the intrepid and dauntless spirits bolted within its walls, were left to commune in peace and solitude and seek the needed rest.

While confined there, they lay upon white oak logs that had been hewn. Their food was very poor. They aver that poison was administered to them three or four times, and even *human flesh* was given them to eat.

After being confined there some time, Sidney Rigdon was released on bail, and made his escape to Illinois.

Sometime in the following April, the other prisoners were taken to Davies County. They there got a change of venue to Boone County, for which place they started; but on the way there the door was opened for their escape. They improved their opportunity, and, in the course of nine or ten days, arrived safely in Quincy, Adams County, Illinois.

In that vicinity, they joined their families and found that, in view of Boggs' order for their extermination or expulsion, the majority of the Saints had already made their escape from Missouri, and found refuge in different localities in Illinois; but the main portion were settled in Adams and adjacent Counties.

In a paper furnished by Hyrum Smith, is the following:

"Governor Boggs and Generals Clark, Lucas, Wilson and Gillum, also Austin A. King, have committed treasonable acts against the citizens of Missouri, and did violate the Constitution of the United States, and also the Constitution and laws of the State of Missouri, and did exile and expel, at the point of the bayonet, some twelve or fourteen thousand inhabitants of the State, and did murder some three or four hundred of men, women and children in cold blood, in the most horrid and cruel manner possible. And the whole of it was caused by religious bigotry and persecution, and because the 'Mormons' dared to worship Almighty God according to the dictates of their own conscience, and agreeably to His divine will, as revealed in the scriptures of eternal truth."

Doubtless, all the murders that were committed in Jackson County, and from that time until the final expulsion from the State, are included in this estimate.

---

## CHAPTER IV.

SAINTS TAKE REFUGE IN ILLINOIS—COMMERCE SELECTED AS A GATHERING PLACE—CONGRESS AND VAN BUREN APPEALED TO FOR REDRESS OF WRONGS—VAN BUREN'S DISGRACEFUL REPLY—NAUVOO INCORPORATED—HYRUM SMITH MADE PATRIARCH—JOSEPH SMITH AGAIN ARRESTED—TRIED BEFORE STEPHEN A. DOUGLASS—DISCHARGED—A PROPHECY—BOGGS' AFFIDAVIT—AVOIDS ARREST—KIDNAPPED AT DIXON—BRUTAL TREATMENT BY REYNOLDS AND WILSON—SCENE AT PAWPAW GROVE—FRIENDS IN NAUVOO AROUSED—SCOUR THE COUNTRY IN SEARCH OF JOSEPH—FIND HIM AND RETURN TO NAUVOO—AN OVATION—KIDNAPPERS ENTERTAINED AS GUESTS—FURTHER EFFORTS OF REYNOLDS AND WILSON TO CAUSE TROUBLE.

THE desire to gather together, and not scatter abroad, has existed in the bosoms of the Saints ever since the Church was organized. The true doctrines of Christ tend to bind together the hearts of His people, that they may live in unision and be enabled, by a close proximity of dwelling, to better appreciate each other's worth, and do the will of God.

Hence, those who are baptized for the remission of their sins and receive the Holy Spirit by the imposition of hands by those holding authority, are impressed with a love for all the human race, and more especially for those who are made partakers of "like precious faith." When the Elders travel to foreign climes and testify in the cottages of the humble, and carry conviction to those who occupy the higher ranks of society, whether they dwell upon the islands of the sea or where the monarch's throne is panoplied with the insignias of imperial sway, with one accord and by an involuntary impulse, that infusion of the divine unction promptly lights within the minds of the converts its taper of love, and turns their faces Zionward.

When the Saints found themselves in Illinois, though grateful for a temporary refuge from the scenes of rapine, chains and death, which had fallen upon them like a desolating tempest, they were necessarily in a scattered condition. But their scattering was the result of those satanic machinations which were first exerted in the spirit world when Christ was the chosen champion to redeem fallen man, and which have been ever exerted on the earth to forestall and nullify every effort that has been made to establish that kingdom which Jehovah decreed should come forth in the last days and stand forever.

When the great Prophet of the last days was permitted to throw off his chains and step forth in freedom upon the soil of Illinois, his inspired mind took in the situation at a glance. The spirit that ever dictated him, now directed his course to take those steps necessary to bind up the broken hearts, and heal the wounded spirits, of the robbed and hunted and exiled pilgrims, who had fled from the tyranny of Boggs and his merciless coadjutors.

He sought for a place where they might obtain land and gather together, in hopes that in Illinois, then so generous and hospitable, the blessings guaranteed in the American Constitution might be enjoyed by them unmolested.

After a short season of enquiry and travel, he was enabled to find and secure such a place. Commerce, Hancock County, was the one selected. It was situated on the eastern shore of the Mississippi. For some distance back from the river the land was rather level, but finally quite a prominent but gradual rise occurred; and then an undulating stretch of country swept back past a strip of woods, and out into the more rolling prairie, on to Carthage, and still farther beyond. The Father of Waters swept around the western limits of the city, with its broad silvery-like sheen bending to the southern edge, as if there, to bid one last adieu before flowing onward through its picturesque banks, down to its junction with the turbid Missouri, and from thence still farther down, at last to lose its identity in "the dark blue sea." On the opposite shore was the village of Montrose, and then the hills and prairie lands of Iowa stretched onward towards the west, beautiful to behold when bedecked with the diurnal gorgeousness of the setting sun.

Here a city was surveyed and thither flocked the joyful Saints, once more to build homes and erect anew their altars of worship.

In the beginning there were some hindrances to be encountered. One of these was that, for a season, the location proved to be unhealthy. Much suffering was endured from ague and fever.

A general Conference of the Church was held at Commerce, on the 5th of October, 1839, at which that place was selected as a Stake of Zion, and a place for the gathering of the Saints. Also, Joseph Smith, Sidney Rigdon and Elias Higbee were appointed to go to the city of Washington to lay before Congress the wrongs which had been inflicted upon the Saints in Missouri. They started on their mission the 29th of October, accompanied by O. P. Rockwell and Doctor Robert H. Foster.

The Prophet Joseph Smith and Brother Higbee arrived in Washington the 28th of November, in advance of the other three, who were detained a few days at Philadelphia, owing to the sickness of Elder Rigdon. The next day they had an interview with President Martin Van Buren. At a subsequent interview, after Joseph had fully laid the matter of the grievances of the Saints before his excellency, Van Buren answered: "*Gentlemen, your cause is just, but I can do nothing for you; if I take up for you, I shall lose the vote of Missouri.*"

"About four hundred and ninety-one persons held claims against Missouri, which Joseph had presented to Congress. These claims amounted, in all, to one million, three hundred and eighty-one thousand and forty-four dollars and fifty-one and a half cents. But they were not all. There was a multitude of similar bills which were to be presented, and respecting which Joseph said, 'if not settled immediately, they will ere long amount to a handsome' sum, increasing by compound interest.'"

The name of Commerce was soon dropped and Nauvoo, which sigifies "beautiful," was substituted in its stead.

On the 3rd, 4th and 5th of October, 1840, a general Conference was held, at which it was resolved to build a House of the Lord at Nauvoo.

"Joseph exerted himself to obtain a charter from the Legislature of the State of Illinois for the city of Nauvoo. He had a charter drawn up, which was, to use his own words, 'for the salvation of the Church, and on principles so broad that every honest man might dwell secure under its protective influence, without distinction of sect or party.' The act incorporating the city was passed by the Legislature, and took effect on the first Monday in February, 1841."

"As Joseph's father had passed away, he being the Patriarch of the Church, it was necessary that another should fill that office. Hyrum Smith, his eldest living son, accordingly received the appointment and was ordained to act in that position. This made a vacancy in the First Presidency, of which quorum Hyrum was a member, and William Law was, by revelation, appointed to the place."

"On the first of February the first election was held in Nauvoo for members of the City Council, and on the third of the same month the City Council was organized. John C. Bennett was elected Mayor. Joseph was elected one of the Councilors. He presented several bills to the Council, among the rest one for an ordinance organizing the Nauvoo Legion, which passed the same day. On the fourth, steps were taken to organize the Legion, and Joseph was elected Lieutenant General of the Nauvoo Legion. The Legion, at its organization, was comprised of six companies."

On the sixth of April, 1841, the corner stones for the Temple were laid.

Notwithstanding a considerable time had elapsed after the Church had left Missouri, and, by their exit, had complied to the utmost with her governor's wicked requirements, still that blood-thirsty Nero was not content. Joseph and Hyrum Smith, and others, had been confined in her jails, endured the jeers and menaces of the vulgar rabble, tasted poison, had human flesh offered them to eat, and worn the iron manacles for six months; yet it appeared that all this was not enough.

On June 5th, 1841, at a hotel in Bear Creek, twenty-eight miles south of Nauvoo, Joseph was arrested by the sheriff of Adams County, Thomas King, and Thomas Jasper, with an officer from Missouri. At Quincy, he obtained a writ of *habeas corpus*, and came before Judge Stephen A. Douglass for hearing, at Monmouth, Warren County, June 9th. Much excitement prevailed at the commencement of the proceedings.

"A young lawyer from Missouri volunteered to plead against Joseph, and he tried his best to convict him. He had not spoken many minutes when he turned sick, requested to be excused by the court, and went out of the house vomiting.

"His language was so violent that the judge was twice under the necessity of ordering him to be silent. Joseph's lawyers stood up manfully and honorably in his defense. They spoke well, and O. H. Browning, who was afterwards a member of President Johnson's Cabinet as Secretary of the Interior, made a powerful plea, in which he told what he, himself, had seen at Quincy, when the Saints were driven out of Missouri; and his words were so touching that his listeners could not refrain from tears, and even Judge Douglass and most of the officers wept.

"In the evening Brother Amasa Lyman preached a brilliant discourse in the Court House, on the first principles of the gospel, which very much changed the feelings of the people.

"The next morning, June 10th, Judge Douglass delivered his opinion on the case. It was that Joseph should be liberated. He was discharged that forenoon. This was a triumph for him, and he felt very thankful to the Lord that he had once more been delivered from the clutches of his cruel persecutors. He and his company, numbering about sixty men, reached Nauvoo on the 11th, and he was received by the Saints with great gladness."

On August 6th, 1842, Joseph delivered the following prophecy, as recorded in his history:

"I prophesied that the Saints would continue to suffer much affliction, and would be driven to the Rocky Mountains; many would apostatize, others would be put to death by our persecutors, or lose their lives in consequence of exposure or disease, and some of you will live to go and assist in making settlements and building cities, and see the Saints become a mighty people in the midst of the Rocky Mountains."

Boggs continued to thirst for the Prophet's blood, and on his affidavit, that Joseph Smith was "accessory before the fact to an assault" made upon him "with intent to kill," by some person whom he supposed to be O. P. Rockwell, a requisition was sent by Governor Reynolds to Carlin, the governor of Illinois, for Joseph's arrest, in connection with that of O. P. Rockwell.

Joseph knew that this was a scheme got up by Boggs and his mobocratic associates to again deprive him of liberty and get him into their clutches, that they might have the privilege of accomplishing, by assassination, what they had failed to effect by any form of law.

Consequently, he secluded himself, and kept from his pursuers all knowledge of his whereabouts. However, sickness in his family led him, upon one or two occasions, to visit his home, where he at one time only escaped those in pursuit, by passing out of the back door as they entered the house in front. On one occasion he went to the public congregation, where he preached a powerful discourse, and then retired again to his retreat.

About this time Governor Carlin's term of office expired, and Thomas Ford was inaugurated in his place.

"On the 9th of December, 1842, Willard Richards, Heber C. Kimball, William Clayton and a number of other brethren, started to Springfield, the capital of the State of Illinois, to present testimony to the governor, that Joseph was in Illinois at the time Boggs was shot. As he was in Illinois at the time, he could not be a fugitive from the justice of Missouri." Ford being in doubt as to his right to interfere with the action of his predecessor in the matter, "submitted the case and all the papers relating thereto to six of the judges of the supreme court. They were unanimous in the opinion that the requisition from Missouri was illegal and insufficient to cause Joseph's arrest. Ford, under the circumstances, declined to act in the premises and advised Joseph to have a judicial investigation. Accordingly, Joseph submitted to an arrest at Nauvoo, on the 26th of December. Joseph went immediately to Springfield, and his trial was commenced before Judge Pope, January 4, 1843. The result was, that on the day following, Judge Pope delivered his decision and Joseph was discharged.

While Joseph was at Springfield he mingled freely with the people and the leading men of the State. His appearance and teachings removed the prejudice which had previously existed, and he was soon treated with the utmost respect. Elders Orson Hyde and John Taylor preached in the State House, and their discourses, also, had a very pacific influence.

All this did not discourage the old Missouri mobbers, nor induce them to desist from their wicked persecutions against the peace and life of this just and innocent man.

In the month of June following, Joseph and his wife, Emma, were visiting her sister, Mrs. Wasson, near Dixon, Lee County, Iowa. On the 23rd of that month, the following disgraceful and brutal scene took place:

"On the 23rd, two men were at Dixon trying to hire a man and team. They said they were 'Mormon' Elders and wanted to see the Prophet. They obtained the team and drove up to Mr. Wasson's while the family were at dinner. They told the same story there: that they were 'Mormon' Elders and wanted to see 'Brother Joseph.' Joseph was in the yard going to the barn, when one of them stepped to the end of the house and saw him. He spoke to Joseph in a very uncouth and ungentlemanly manner, and the other one stepped up to him and collared him. They lied when they said they were 'Mormon' Elders. One of them was Joseph H. Reynolds, sheriff of Jackson County, Missouri, and the other was Constable Harmon T. Wilson, of Carthage, Illinois. They presented their cocked pistols to Joseph's breast, and Reynolds cried out with big oaths that if he stirred an inch he would shoot him. Joseph inquired what the meaning of all this was. No satisfactory answer was given; but the oaths and threats were repeated. Joseph told them 'I am not afraid of your shooting; I am not afraid to die.' He then bared his breast and told them to shoot away. Said he, 'I have endured so much oppression, I am weary of life; and kill me if you please. I am a strong man, however, and with my own natural weapons could soon level both of you; but if you have any legal process to serve, I am at all times subject to law, and shall not offer resistance.' Reynolds swore again that if Joseph said another word he would shoot him. To this Joseph replied that he could shoot away, he was not afraid of his pistols. By this time Brother Stephen Markham walked towards them. When they saw him coming, they turned their pistols from Joseph to him, and threatened his life if he came any nearer. He paid no attention to their threats; but continued to advance nearer. Seeing they could not stop him by their threats they turned their pistols on Joseph again. They jammed them against his sides, and holding their fingers on the triggers, ordered Brother Markham to stand still, or they would shoot Joseph through. As Brother Markham was advancing rapidly towards them, Joseph said to him, 'you are not going to resist the officers, are you, Brother Markham?' He replied, 'No, not if they are officers; I know the law too well for that.'"

It would be gratifying here to relate the circumstances, in detail, that followed this unceremonious and illegal arrest. The want of room alone prevents their insertion. Suffice it to state that the prisoner was persistently abused by his captors, who attempted to run him into Missouri before he could obtain any legal process for his benefit. They did not want to give him time to procure a change of clothes or bid his wife good by.

They several times threatened to shoot Joseph, who asked them why they did not shoot, if they wanted to, and not so often threaten to do so. They punched him in his sides, with their pistols, until his flesh was discolored for about eighteen inches in circumference. They ordered fresh horses to expedite their flight with him and get him out of Illinois. "But Joseph saw a person, and he shouted to him through a window that he was falsely imprisoned, and wanted a lawyer."

Two lawyers came and the door was banged in their faces. This occurred at Dixon, where several persons "gathered around the hotel door and gave Reynolds to understand that if that was their mode of doing business in Missouri, they had another mode of doing it in Dixon."

A writ of *habeas corpus* was obtained, made returnable before Judge John D. Caton of Ottawa. A writ was also sued out against Reynolds and Wilson for private damage and false imprisonment, claiming $10,000 damages. On their way to Ottawa, they stopped for the night at Pawpaw Grove. The landlord and others noticed the abuse practiced towards Joseph by his captors.

Early next morning the room was filled with the citizens of the place, anxious to see the "Mormon" Prophet and hear him preach. Reynolds could not stand this, and, pointing to Joseph said: "I wish you to understand this man is my prisoner, and I want you to disperse: you must not gather round here in this way."

"Just as he said this a Mr. David Town, an aged gentleman, who was lame and carried a large hickory walking stick, stepped towards Reynolds, and bringing his stick down upon the floor, cursed him, and said:

"'We'll learn you to come here and interrupt gentlemen. Sit down there (pointing to a very low chair,) and sit still. Don't open your head till General Smith gets through talking. If you never learned manners in Missouri. we'll teach you that gentlemen are not to be imposed upon by a nigger-driver. You can *not* kidnap men here. There's a committee in this grove that will sit on your case; and. sir, it is the highest tribunal in the United States, as *from its decision there is no appeal.*'

"Reynolds quietly sat down, and Joseph addressed the assembly for an hour-and-a-half on the subject of marriage. The company requested that he should speak upon that subject."

"Learning that Judge Caton was on a visit to New York, the company, among whom were Joseph's three lawyers, returned to Dixon. Here Joseph was again locked up in a room and guarded."

In the meantime, William Clayton had taken passage on the steamboat *Amaranth* down the Mississippi river to Nauvoo, who conveyed to Hyrum Smith information of his brother Joseph's situation. Hyrum acted with great promptness and energy, and forthwith a company of over three hundred men volunteered, and from their number about one hundred and seventy-five men were selected and started the same evening, on horseback.

As soon afterwards as possible, other companies of horsemen started in different directions through the State to intercept any company of kidnappers that might attempt to run him into Missouri. Also the Steamboat *Maid of Iowa*, with Elder John Taylor, and others, on board, steamed down the Mississippi and up the Illinois river to Peru, then back to Nauvoo, to have an eye on steamboats and detect, if possible, any move that might be made to take Joseph to Missouri by such conveyance.

The absence of Judge Caton made it necessary that the writ of *habeas corpus* which Joseph had obtained should be renewed, which was done and made "returnable before the nearest tribunal in the Fifth Judicial District authorized to hear and determine writs of *habeas corpus*. This was served immediately on Reynolds and Wilson by the sheriff of Lee County, which made them his prisoners.

Afterwards, at the proper time, Joseph told his lawyers that the Municipal Court of the City of Nauvoo was the nearest tribunal to hear and determine writs of *habeas corpus*. They examined the law and found he was correct.

Joseph started from Dixon on the 26th of June. When about forty-five miles from that place, he began to meet the advance of the company from Nauvoo, when he said: "I am not going to Missouri this time. These are my boys." The joy that was felt by Joseph and his accompanying friends at this meeting was beyond description; but his brutal captors were seized with trembling. The company began to travel as much as possible, in the direction of Nauvoo, which alarmed Reynolds and Wilson, who swore "they would never go to Nauvoo alive." The sheriff demanded their arms. They remonstrated, but finally delivered them to the sheriff.

Some of the facts as to Joseph's position and prospects for reaching Nauvoo were expressed to that city, and, on the 30th day of June, 1843:

"The Nauvoo Brass and Martial Bands, and Joseph's wife—who had proceeded to Nauvoo after his arrest—his brother Hyrum, and a number of the principal inhabitants in carriages, started to meet him. By the time the company met Joseph it had swelled to a considerable size, and with the company that was with him (one hundred and forty men on horseback) the procession became an imposing one. When the company from the city came up, Joseph said he thought he would ride a little easier, and he got out of the buggy in which he had been riding. He embraced his wife and his brother Hyrum, who shed tears of joy at his return; and in this they were not alone, the most of the great company did the same. Joseph mounted his favorite horse, 'Old Charley,' which had been brought out to meet him, the band struck up 'Hail Columbia,' and the procession marched towards the city."

Joseph was received by the Saints in Nauvoo with an ovation. His entry to the city is described as follows:

"His march was like that of a conqueror. The scene was an exceedingly interesting one. As the procession neared the city the streets were lined on both sides with the people, whose faces beamed with joy at seeing their beloved Prophet and leader once more safe. Amid their cheers, the firing of cannons and the most intense enthusiasm Joseph marched into the city. So great was the eagerness to see him and get close to him that it required a number of men to keep the streets open for the procession to pass. Joseph's mother was at his house awaiting his arrival, and tears of joy rolled down her aged cheeks as she beheld and embraced her beloved son, and welcomed him once more in safety from the hands of his enemies."

Joseph made his captors his guests. Many of his friends were seated at his table, at the head of which were placed Reynolds and Wilson, who were served by his wife, whom they had cruelly refused to allow Joseph to see when they arrested him. This was returning good for evil—"heaping coals of fire on their heads"—and had the effect, no doubt, of presenting a mirror before them in which they could see reflected their own little meanness. While thus partaking of the hospitalities of Joseph's table, the writer heard Wilson, in an undertone, remark to Reynolds: "I feel like we have got into the rong pew."

A full hearing was had, July 1st, before the Municipal Court, and Joseph was discharged.

Joseph's lawyers—Walker, Patrick, Southwick and Backman—addressed the court and exhorted the Saints "to stand for their rights—stand or fall, sink or swim, live or die."

Reynolds and Wilson hastened to Carthage and began to incite the people to mobocracy.

"The lawyers mentioned made an affidavit to the effect that no violence or threats had been made use of towards Reynolds and Wilson either on the journey to or after their arrival at Nauvoo, and that they came to Nauvoo voluntarily and were in no danger of violence, etc. This affidavit was drawn up to contradict the lies which Reynolds and Wilson had told to excite prejudice against Joseph and the Saints and to make the public believe that their prisoner had been taken from their custody unfairly, by threats of violence. In fact, scarcely had this affidavit been signed when word came to Nauvoo from Carthage that these villainous men were stirring up the people to mobocracy, and were about to send a petition to Governor Ford for a *posse* to retake Joseph. Reynolds and Wilson had filed their affidavits that Col. Markham had, with armed force, taken Joseph out of their hands. The citizens of Nauvoo immediately made out a petition to the Governor, praying him not to issue any more writs against Joseph; also a remonstrance against the Carthage proceedings. A transcript of the trial before the Municipal Court, and various other documents throwing light upon Joseph's case, were delivered to his lawyers, with instructions to see Governor Ford immediately."

"Reynolds, when he was foiled in his scheme to carry Joseph into Missouri, presented a petition to Governor Ford for a detachment of militia to be detailed to assist him in retaking Joseph. Ford, in the meantime, however, had received the remonstrance and affidavits of the people of Nauvoo and Joseph's lawyers, which were all adverse to Reynolds' request. The lawyers were influential men, and Walker was a member of the Whig party—Ford, himself, was a Democrat—and if he did not act with some degree of fairness, they might expose him, and damage him, politically. He did not dare, therefore, to grant Reynolds' petition without further investigation. He sent a messenger—a Mr. Braman—to Nauvoo, for a copy of all the testimony that was given in the case before the Municipal Court and affidavits concerning the expulsion of the Saints from Missouri. Upon his report the Governor decided to take no action in response to Reynolds' demand."

Governor Ford's refusal to grant Reynolds' demand in the matter of calling out a detachment of militia to assist in retaking Joseph, was used by the Whig party as political capital, in the campaign then in progress for members of Congress, and those with mobocratic proclivities, in both parties, were much disconcerted and incensed.

The mobocrats from Missouri, especially Reynolds, felt mortified at being so signally defeated in the scheme to carry Joseph back to Missouri as a prisoner. Considerable censure, from that quarter, was attached to Ford's refusal to comply with Reynolds' demand for militia, and in an explanatory letter written by him to the Governor of Missouri, Ford

"contended that the laws of the State of Illinois had been fully exercised in the matter. A writ was issued for Joseph's apprehension; he was apprehended, and duly delivered by the officer of the State of Illinois to the agent of the State of Missouri appointed to receive him. No process, officer, or authority of Illinois had been resisted or interfered with. Governor Ford said he had fully executed the duty which the laws imposed upon him, and there had been no resistance either in the writ issued for the arrest of Joseph or in the person of the officer appointed to apprehend him. There had been no warlike array in the proceedings of Joseph and his friends, no exhibition of arms, and no actual force of an illegal character. Everything had been done on his part which the law warranted him in doing; and he ended by saying, that 'in no one aspect of the case can I consider the present an extreme emergency, warranting a call for the militia, according to the provision of the law of the State.'"

This utter failure to get Joseph into Missouri, also greatly exasperated the mobbers of Hancock and adjacent Counties, and a meeting was held at Carthage, the 19th of August, 1833, and a committee of six appointed to draft resolutions which were presented to an adjourned meeting held on the 6th of September.

---

## CHAPTER V.

### REVIEW OF JOSEPH SMITH'S CHARACTER—A CANDIDATE FOR THE PRESIDENCY OF THE U. S.—"EXPOSITOR" ISSUED—DECLARED A NUISANCE—ABATED BY ORDER OF CITY COUNCIL—EFFORTS TO TAKE JOSEPH SMITH TO CARTHAGE FOR TRIAL ON CHARGE OF RIOT—HIS OBJECTIONS TO GOING THERE—IMPRESSION THAT HE WOULD BE MURDERED—THE GOVERNOR INSISTS UPON IT—JOSEPH SUBMITS.

IN the preceding chapters reference has been made to some of the more noted and prominent occurrences which have marked the career of the remarkable man whose memory is, to-day, cherished by thousands of devoted followers of the doctrines he enunciated.

As has been seen, in every position he occupied before his enemies, his attitudes and words were most fearlessly assumed. As his stature was erect and commanding, so were his language and doctrines bold and dignified. His words were vigorous in rebuke, when addressed to the wicked rabble, who quailed under their potency. But into the hearts of the meek and humble they fell with gentleness, as night-dews are distilled among the blooming flowers, to refresh and render them still more beautiful as the effulgent morning darts thither the kisses of its earliest sunbeams.

With a strong and manly hand he grappled with the oppressor and tore away the subtlety of his covering. To the demagogue he presented the mirror which reflected his deformity, that he might behold himself in his true light. The politician was, by him, pointed to a higher plane of constitutional attainments than was before considered in his category.

Priests stood as dumb mutes before him, or, for want of argument, incited the populace to violence. That the Holy Spirit does not permeate the dogmas and forms of religion which the sectarian creeds inculcate, is rendered plain by comparison with the pure gospel which God commanded Joseph Smith to proclaim.

The proofs of his sincerity are most convincing. They are portrayed in the inclinations of his boyhood to seek for light from the divine source whence it emanates in purity; and later still in the fortitude with which he withstood priestcraft when the truths of the gospel had made their inceptive impress upon his young heart. They may be traced in the earnestness with which he pushed forward his great mission to man. They are discerned in the evident unselfishness associated with his every movement. They shine forth from prisons and are heralded in the rattling chains that deprived him of liberty. The same quality is attested by the numerous acts of self-denial that mark his pathway through life, as well as by the invincibility of his doctrines.

Is it possible for him to have given any higher evidence that his mission was divinely inspired? Reader, follow him a little farther to the culmination—where he towers to the zenith of his greatness—and it will be plain that mortal man could not do more.

The Savior said, "Greater love hath no man than this, that a man lay down his life for his friends." Joseph and Hyrum Smith gave this proof of their love.

All that remains to be enacted by Joseph Smith, the Prophet, while in the flesh, will speedily be consummated. Feeble indeed is the writer's pen to do justice to the fleeting moments of time which remain. Therein will the unflinching integrity of the man be brought to a test. Dearer than worldly fame and its heights of power, were the inspired convictions of his soul, and soon he lays them all upon the altar of sacrifice to be cemented with his blood.

Let us enquire into a few more of the immediate causes which led to this tragic issue.

Aside from the excitements and troubles that existed in Hancock County, there were powerful influences and jealousies in the circle of some of the leading men at the capital of the nation. On what grounds? They grew, in part, out of the presidential canvass that was in progress during the early part of the summer of 1844. Henry Clay, Martin Van Buren and John C. Calhoun, were before the country as candidates for the high office of chief executive. For important reasons, neither of these distinguished gentlemen were acceptable to the Latter-day Saints.

Van Buren had declared that the grievances of our people were well founded, but said he could do nothing for us.

Calhoun declared the power of the federal government to be so "limited" and "specific" that the wholesale robberies and murders of mobocrats could not be brought within the scope of its jurisdiction.

When Joseph addressed a letter of enquiry to Henry Clay, asking: "What will be your rule of action relative to us as a people, should fortune favor your ascension to the chief magistracy?" that gentleman's position was found to be entirely non-committal. His political principles were not such as Joseph and his friends could endorse.

There was not a man brought forward in that campaign that could be acceptable to the Saints, for not one of them had the courage or honesty to say to them: There is power in the American Congress; there is vitality in the country's laws; there is patriotism in the people; the federal government has jurisdiction to see that the Constitution is preserved inviolate, and the wrongs of which you complain shall be investigated.

Under these circumstances, the name of Joseph Smith was placed in the *Times and Seasons* as a candidate for the office of President of the United States, and that of Sidney Rigdon for Vice President.

This was considered a bold step, but the political exigencies of the times seemed to require it. He was a native born citizen of "the home of the free." His ancestors were among the early patriots, whose valor achieved the American Independence. The Constitution made him eligible for that position, and his principles and aims were pre-eminently superior to those of his opponents, as was made plain in his published "Powers and Policy of the Government."

## JEALOUSY OF JOSEPH'S ENEMIES. 51

His being a candidate was especially distasteful to Van Buren and Benton; so much so, that there were good grounds for the belief that an understanding was had between them and the Governors of Missouri and Illinois, and from them down through some of the State and County officers, that Joseph was getting too much power and influence, and his career must come to a close before the end of the campaign. The truth of this cannot be positively vouched for by the writer, but it is believed. At all events, something seemed to change the pacific policy of Governor Ford, which is easily discerned by any who read his letters and public documents of those times. It was said that Benton promised the vote of Missouri to Van Buren upon condition that he would wipe out the "Mormons," if elected.

Joseph's enemies in Nauvoo were also filled with enmity and jealousy towards him because of this candidateship. They began to see that his popularity was far greater, in different parts of the States, than they had anticipated. They feared he might be successful at some subsequent time, if not then, and they could not bear the thoughts that there should be any probability of his advancement to that or any other position of distinction in the Government. They dreaded his noble principles and independence of character, knowing that wherever he might hold power, their own chances for preferment would be hopeless, at least while they continued to be corrupt.

Of course, they affiliated with every element opposed to Joseph, and, being rank apostates, resident there, they were the better enabled to give direction to the plans concocted against him—thus causing the envenomed arrows of the combined enemy to be aimed with deadly purpose.

In addition to their viciousness of character, in many things they calulated with some shrewdness and planned to make a show of consistency in their movements. They knew the element that composed the society of Hancock. They understood the prestige conceded to the press by the American public. They knew also Joseph's character, and that establishing a libelous and venal newspaper in Nauvoo would not be agreeable to him. Hence a paper of that class was started, with the understanding that if Joseph and the local authorities opposed its continuance, their opposition might be used as a very good pretext for the commencement of active movements against Joseph's election as well as his life.

They issued their prospectus about the 10th of May. Among the things they proposed to advocate were:

"The unconditional repeal of the city charter of Nauvoo, to restrain and correct the abuses of the UNIT POWER, to ward off the rod which is held over the devoted heads of the citizens of Nauvoo and the surrounding country, to advocate unmitigated DISOBEDIENCE TO POLITICAL REVELATION, to advocate and exercise the freedom of speech in Nauvoo, independent of the ordinance abridging the same—to give toleration to every man's religious sentiments and sustain ALL in worshiping their God according to the monitions of their consciences, as guaranteed by the Constitution of our country, and to oppose, with uncompromising hostility any UNION OF CHURCH AND STATE or any preliminary steps tending to the same," etc.

The *Expositor* was issued on June 7th. Its columns teemed with vituperative abuse of Joseph and his friends. That it was the fixed purpose of its managers to continue that defamatory course, was evident from the matter contained in its columns and in their private admissions. They aimed to attack the characters of many respectable citizens of both sexes. The tone of the sheet was vulgar, scurrilous, and untruthful. The people felt themselves outraged.

On the 10th of June, the city council investigated the matter thoroughly and declared the *Expositor* a nuisance, and, with united vote, passed the following:

*Bill for Removing of the Press of the 'Nauvoo Expositor.'*

"Resolved by the City Council of the City of Nauvoo, that the printing office from whence issues the *Nauvoo Expositor* is a public nuisance; and also of said *Nauvoo Expositors* which may be or exist in said establishment; and the mayor is instructed to cause said establishment and papers to be removed without delay, in such manner as he shall direct.

"Passed June 10th, 1844. GEO. W. HARRIS,

"W. RICHARDS, Recorder. President *pro tem*."

"Higbee immediately went to Carthage and made a complaint before the justice of the peace, swearing to an affidavit that Joseph and seventeen other brethren had committed a riot, alleging that, with force and violence, they had broken into the Nauvoo *Expositor* printing office and unlawfully burned and destroyed the printing press, type and other property of the same. The name of the justice before whom this complaint was made, was Thomas Morrison, and he sent a constable with a writ to Nauvoo, to arrest Joseph. The writ stated that the officer was to bring the persons charged in it 'before me (Morrison) or some other justice of the peace, to answer the premises, and further to be dealt with according to law.'

"When he had finished reading the writ, Joseph referred the officer who bore it, to that clause, and said: 'We are ready to go to trial before Esquire Johnson or any justice in Nauvoo.' At this, the constable was very angry, and he swore he would carry them to Carthage before Morrison, who had issued the writ. Joseph asked him if he intended to break the law, and called upon all present to witness that he then offered himself to go immediately before the nearest justice of the peace. His brother Hyrum offered to do the same. Joseph felt so indignant at the officer's abuse, that he was determined to take out a *habeas corpus*, and petitioned the municipal court of the city of Nauvoo, to grant him the benefit of that writ, and, on the afternoon of the same day, he appeared before that court, and the case was examined. It was 'decided by the court that Joseph Smith had acted under proper authority in destroying the establishment of the Nauvoo *Expositor*, on the 10th inst. ; that his orders were executed in an orderly and judicious manner, without noise or tumult; that this was a malicious prosecution on the part of F. M. Higbee; and that said Higbee pay costs of suit, and that Joseph Smith be honorably discharged from the accusations of the writ, and go hence without delay.'

"The other brethren were arrested the next day, and they also petitioned for and obtained a writ of *habeas corpus*, and were tried before the municipal court on that day; and, after witnesses had been examined as in the case of Joseph, they were all honorably discharged from the accusations and arrests. The court decided that Higbee pay the costs of the suits."

Joseph's enemies made all the capital they could in consequence of this, by informing Governor Ford that he had resisted the writ from the circuit court, etc.

Great excitement spread through Hancock and adjacent Counties. Inflammatory speeches were made by designing politicans and lawyers. The "Mormons," they said, had made war upon the liberty of the press, and their leaders ought to be killed and the others driven from the country.

The press and office belonging to the Saints in Jackson County was destroyed by a MOB, and the mobocrats of Missouri applauded the occurrence and the governor of that State sanctioned it. And the mobocrats of Illinois, at the time of these troubles, sanctioned it also, by their deeds, and said it was all right because that was a "Mormon" press. At the same time they inflamed the public mind to the utmost of their ability, because a legally constituted body had the manliness to abate, as a nuisance, a press, the avowed object of which was to take from the citizens of a city duly incorporated, their chartered rights.

It has been said that "the press is the lever that moves the world." Also, that "the pen is mightier than the sword." Whether these assertions be fully true or otherwise, every person of intelligence must acknowledge that they are mighty agents whether employed either "for weal or for woe." In the American society, by the popular will, the career of the press and the pen, as well as speech, pursue their various missions with but little restriction. This is right and quite proper when the causes in which they are employed are just, honest, lawful and patriotic. It is to be regretted that this is not always the case. They often descend from their legitimate elevations to the slums of vice and defamation, and, in suits brought for libel, damages are sometimes awarded by the courts. But notwithstanding there are provisions for legal redress, the press and the pen too often combine their influence for evil, and the honest citizen as well as States and nations are abridged in the exercise of their just rights.

The case before us now, is one where the press was venal and corrupt. Its owners and writers were wicked and vindictive. They stooped from the height where they should have watched the approach of the invading foe, and hurled their envenomed darts at their neighbors and fellow citizens, for whom they had for years made protestations of friendship, and with whom they had even communed at the sacramental table. And because those neighbors, whose homes and peace were thus invaded, would not tamely brook their abuse, they sought to inflame the popular mind with motives of violence, that their homes might be committed to the flames, their liberties taken from them and their lives be given to the assassin. This they accomplished.

"This paper was published on the 7th of June; twenty days afterwards, Joseph and Hyrum were cruelly murdered in Carthage Jail, by a mob. It was through the schemes of these wicked men who made such pious pretentions, that the Prophet Joseph and his brother Hyrum were brought there, and those apostates were accessory to their murder. Within three weeks after they wrote these plausible words, their garments were dripping with the blood of innocence."

"Every effort was made by the enemies of the Saints, after the *Expositor* was declared a nuisance, to fan the flames of persecution and to form combinations to drive and exterminate them. In some parts, they threatend to drive or kill every Latter-day Saint who did not deny the faith and cease to believe that Joseph was a prophet of God. They also threatened to use violence to those who were not Latter-day Saints, if they did not take up arms to help them drive the Church out of the country. Those whom they could not persuade to join them in their schemes, they tried to frighten by their threats. They told men of this class that they must join them, or leave the country, or give their arms to them. One of the leading spirits of this work of persecution was one Levi Williams, a colonel of militia, and a Baptist preacher. With all his pretentions to religion, he was a great villain. Robbery, house-burning, murder and every other act of violence, he thought perfectly right, so long as the Latter-day Saints were the victims. To accomplish the destruction of the Saints, he was willing to adopt any measure, however wicked or violent. There were many others who were like him. They acted upon the idea that it was no disgrace to shoot a 'Mormon;' that he had no rights which they should respect. Where they had the power, they were very violent and abusive; but they were always careful to have the largest number on their side when they made an attack on any person or settlement. They visited individuals and those who lived in small settlements, because they were not afraid of meeting equal numbers to resist them. As soon as the help which they expected from Missouri should arrive, they said they should march against Joseph and the city of Nauvoo, capture him and destroy the city. They expected about fifteen hundred or two thousand men from Missouri to help them.

"Joseph was well informed respecting the movements of the mob, and he counseled the brethren to keep cool and prepare their arms for the defense of the city. He had guards posted on all the roads leading out of the city, and, within the city, he had other guards stationed in the streets and on the river bank. This he did in his capacity as Lieutenant-General of the Nauvoo

Legion. He also issued orders to have all the powder and lead in the city secured, and that all the arms should be brought into use, and those which were not used by their owners be put into the hands of those who could use them. Under the circumstances which then existed, these preparations were necessary, for the mob were threatening to march upon the city, and they could only be kept from doing so by the knowledge that the Saints were prepared to give them a warm reception. Joseph, in company with several officers of the Legion, visited the prairie east of Nauvoo and arranged his plans for the defense of the city, and selected the most suitable points at which to meet the mob. He also made arrangements to secure provisions for the city, giving his agent instructions to pledge his farms for that purpose. On the 18th of June, he proclaimed the city of Nauvoo under martial law, and issued the following proclamation:

"To the Marshal of the City of Nauvoo,—

From the newspapers around us, and the current reports as brought in from the surrounding country, I have good reason to fear that a mob is organizing to come upon this city, and plunder and destroy said city, as well as murder the citizens; and by virtue of the authority vested in me as Mayor, and to preserve the city and lives of the citizens, I do hereby declare the said city, within the limits of its corporation, under martial law. The officers, therefore, of the Nauvoo Legion, the police, as well as all others, will strictly see that no persons or property pass in or out of the city without due orders.

JOSEPH SMITH, Mayor."

"Two days previous to the proclamation of martial law, a public meeting was held at which a number of delegates were appointed to go to the different precincts throughout the County to lay a true statement of the condition of affairs at Nauvoo before the people, and to correct the many false reports which had been put in circulation. Joseph, on the same day, in his capacity as Mayor, issued a proclamation, in which he explained, at length, the causes which had led to the *Expositor* being declared a nuisance and destroyed. He also wrote to Governor Ford and sent his letter by the hands of Edward Hunter, Philip B. Lewis and John Bills as messengers. In this letter, he expressed his desire that the Governor would come to Nauvoo in person, with his staff, and investigate the whole difficulty without delay. This he thought would be the best method of restoring peace to the country. With the letter, he sent an affidavit concerning the intentions of the mob.

"All this evidence had, however, but little weight with Governor Ford. He lacked the firmness, decision of character and the sense of justice necessary to maintain order and to enforce the right. He became the tool of the mob, and they managed him, without informing him of all their plans, to suit their purposes. On the 21st of June, he came to Carthage, one of the places where the mob had full sway, and sent an express into Nauvoo to the mayor and city council, requesting them to send out to him one or more well-informed, discreet persons, who could lay before him the city council's version of the difficulty. Elders John Taylor, Willard Richards and Dr. John M. Bernhisel were selected to go. Brothers Taylor and Bernhisel did go, taking with them a number of affidavits, which set forth in great plainness the acts of the mob, and Brother Richards remained to prepare additional documents. The next day, these documents were sent by the hand of Lucien Woodworth, who went in the stead of Dr. Richards. Joseph wrote another long letter to Governor Ford, and sent by him, in which he made many explanations, and repeated his request for the governor to come to Nauvoo. If he would come there the mayor and city council could lay the whole matter before him in its true colors and sustain their statements by an abundance of testimony. But if they had to go to Carthage to do this, they would expose themselves to the power of a mob, filled with fury and a desire to shed blood, a part of whom had already fired several times upon the Saints."

Joseph had been tried twice for abating the *Expositor*, once by the Municipal Court where the case had been brought on a writ of *habeas corpus*, and, secondly, before Daniel H. Wells, a Justice of the Peace. In the letter last referred to, written by Joseph to the Governor at Carthage, he said:

"How it could be possible for them to be tried constitutionally by the same magistrate who first issued the writ, they could not see; for the Constitution expressly says no man shall twice be put in jeopardy of life and limb for the same offense. But, notwithstanding this, he said, they would not hesitate to stand another trial, according to his wish, were it not that they were confident their lives would be in danger. He told Ford he had promised them protection; but, 'at the same time,' said he, 'you have expressed fears that you could not control the mob, in which case we are left to the mercy of the merciless.' He told him further that writs were issued against them in various parts of the country, so that the mob might have the power to drag them from place to place and from court to court, till some blood-thirsty villain could find an opportunity to shoot them. Joseph closed his letter by saying that if anything wrong had been done on the part of himself and others (yet he knew of nothing,) they would make all things right if the Government would give them the opportunity. And he entreated the Governor to disperse the mob, and secure to himself and friends their constitutional privileges, that their lives might not be endangered when they were on trial.

"But Governor Ford was deaf to all reason. He was surrounded by apostates and the worst enemies of the Saints. On his arrival at Carthage, he had ordered the entire mob into service. He heard their imprecations and their threats, and saw their violence and outrageous conduct; but instead of being disgusted with them, they suited him. He adopted, as the truth, every lie and misrepresentation that the mob circulated. The delegates, whom he wished the Mayor and City Council of Nauvoo to send to him, he treated with great rudeness. When they attempted to make the necessary statements and explanations, he suffered them to be interrupted and insulted by the vile crew who were his companions. Even the communications which they brought were read to him in the presence of these villains, who frequently interrupted the reading by their cursing!"

Governor Ford had taken his position at Carthage, and could not be induced by all of Joseph's entreaties to come to Nauvoo and investigate for himself, where Joseph's acts could be fairly investigated. He seemed to be in the plot of the mob to get Joseph dragged to Carthage at all hazards. Joseph no doubt felt and saw that the times were momentous and portended evil towards him. He knew it was his life they sought. He could not with any confidence place himself in their hands. He wanted his most reliable friends with him, and wrote letters to the Twelve, then on missions, to return home. "He was anxious to get Hyrum, his brother, out of the way. Said he: 'I wish I could get Hyrum out of the way, so that he may live to avenge my blood; and I will stay with you and see it out.' But Hyrum could not be moved. If Joseph suffered and died, he was determined to suffer and die with him. Said he to the Prophet: 'Joseph, I cannot leave you.'"

"Joseph remarked to Brother Stephen Markham that, if he and Hyrum were ever taken again, they would be massacred, or he was not a prophet of God. He added: 'I want Hyrum to live to avenge my blood, but he is determined not to leave me.'"

The governor seemed determined that Joseph and Hyrum and the other brethren charged with riot in the matter of the *Expositor* should go to Carthage for trial, notwithstanding they had been twice tried already and acquitted. He sent word that Joseph and Hyrum should be protected by the militia of the State, and, on this assurance, they sent word to the governor that they would come to Carthage and submit to another trial.

## CHAPTER VI.

THE PROPHET'S LAST PUBLIC SPEECH—START FOR CARTHAGE—REMARKS ON PASSING THE TEMPLE AND LEAVING 'SQUIRE WELLS—ORDER FROM THE GOVERNOR TO DELIVER UP THE STATE ARMS—RETURN TO NAUVOO TO HAVE THE ORDER COMPLIED WITH—REACH CARTHAGE AT MIDNIGHT—THE GOVERNOR PLEDGES THE FAITH OF THE STATE FOR THEIR PROTECTION—THE PRISONERS EXHIBITED BEFORE THE TROOPS—JOSEPH'S REMARKS TO OFFICERS WHO VISITED HIM.

UNDER date of June 18, 1844, Joseph says in his history: "About 2 p. m., the Legion was drawn up in the street close by the mansion. I stood in full uniform on the top of the frame of a building.

"Judge Phelps read the *Warsaw Signal* extra of the 17th, wherein all the 'old citizens' were called upon to assist the mob in exterminating the leaders of the Saints and driving away the people.

"I addressed the Legion for about one-and-a-half hours."

The following synopsis of this address was compiled by George A. Smith from the verbal reports of Joseph G. Hovey, William G. Sterrett, Robert Campbell, and many others who heard the Prophet on the occasion:

"It is thought by some that our enemies would be satisfied with my destruction; but I tell you that as soon as they have shed my blood, they will thirst for the blood of every man in whose heart dwells a single spark of the spirit of the fullness of the gospel. The opposition of these men is moved by the spirit of the adversary of all righteousness. It is not only to destroy me, but every man and woman who dares believe the doctrines that God hath inspired me to teach to this generation.

"We have never violated the laws of our country. We have every right to live under their protection, and are entitled to all the privileges guaranteed by our State and national Constitutions. We have turned the barren, bleak prairies and swamps of this State into beautiful towns, farms, and cities, by our industry; and the men who seek our destruction and cry thief, treason, riot, etc., are those who themselves violate the laws, steal and plunder from their neighbors, and seek to destroy the innocent, heralding forth lies to screen themselves from the just punishment of their crimes by bringing destruction upon this innocent people. I call God, angels, and all men to witness that we are innocent of the charges which are heralded forth through the public prints against us by our enemies; and while they assemble together in unlawful mobs to take away our rights and destroy our lives, they think to shield themselves under the refuge of lies which they have thus wickedly fabricated.

"We have forwarded a particular account of all our doings to the Governor. We are ready to obey his commands, and we expect that protection at his hands which we know to be our just due.

"We have taken the counsel of Judge Thomas, and have been tried before a civil magistrate on the charge of riot—not that the law required it, but because the Judge advised it as a precautionary measure, to allay all possible pretext for excitement. We were legally acquitted by Esquire Wells, who is a good judge of law. Had we been before the Circuit, the Supreme, or any other court of law in this State or nation, we should have been acquitted, for we have broken no law.

"Constable Bettisworth comes here with a writ requiring us to go before Mr. Morrison, 'or some other justice of the peace of the county,' to answer to the charge of riot. We acknowledged ourselves his prisoners, and were ready to go before any magistrate in any precinct in this part of the County, or anywhere else where our lives could be protected from the mob who have published the resolutions for our extermination which you have just heard read. This is a privilege the law guarantees to us, and which the writ itself allows. He breaks the law, and refuses us this privilege, declaring that we shall go before Morrison in Carthage, *and no one else*, when he knew that a numerous mob was collected there who are publicly pledged to destroy our lives.

"It was under these circumstances that we availed ourselves of the legal right of the ancient, high, and constitutional privilege of the writ of *habeas corpus*, and were brought before the Municipal Court of this city, and discharged from the illegal detention under which we were held by Constable Bettisworth. All mob-men, priests, thieves, and bogus makers, apostates and adulterers, who combined to destroy this people, now raise the hue and cry throughout the State that we resist the law, in order to raise a pretext for calling together thousands more of infuriated mob-men to murder, destroy, plunder and ravish the innocent.

"We are American citizens. We live upon a soil for the liberties of which our fathers periled their lives and spilt their blood upon the battle-field. Those rights, so dearly purchased, shall not be disgracefully trodden under foot by lawless marauders without at least a noble effort on our part to sustain our liberties.

Will you all stand by me to the death, and sustain, at the peril of your lives, the laws of our country, and the liberties and privileges which our fathers have transmitted unto us, sealed with their sacred blood? ('Aye,' shouted thousands.) He then said—'It is well. If you had not done it, I would have gone out there, (pointing to the west.) and would have raised up a mightier people.'

"I call upon all men, from Maine to the Rocky Mountains, and from Mexico to British America, whose hearts thrill with horror to behold the rights of freemen trampled under foot, to come to the deliverance of this people from the cruel hand of oppression, cruelty, anarchy and misrule to which they have been long made subject. Come, all ye lovers of liberty, break the oppressor's rod, loose the iron grasp of mobocracy, and bring to condign punishment all those who trample under foot the principles of our glorious Constitution and the people's rights." (Drawing his sword, and presenting it to heaven, he said)—"I call God and angels to witness that I have unsheathed my sword with a firm and unalterable determination that this people shall have their legal rights, and be protected from mob violence, or my blood shall be spilt upon the ground like water, and my body consigned to the silent tomb. While I live, I will never tamely submit to the dominion of a cursed mobocracy. I would welcome death rather than submit to this oppression; and it would be sweet, oh, sweet to rest in the grave, rather than submit to this oppression, agitation, annoyance, confusion, and alarm upon alarm, any longer.

"I call upon all friends of truth and liberty to come to our assistance; and may the thunders of the Almighty, and the forked lightnings of heaven, and pestilence, and war, and bloodshed come down on those ungodly men who seek to destroy my life and the lives of this innocent people.

"I do not regard my own life. I am ready to be offered a sacrifice for this people; for what can our enemies do? Only kill the body, and their power is then at an end. Stand firm, my friends; never flinch. Do not seek to save your lives, for he that is afraid to die for the truth will lose eternal life. Hold out to the end, and we shall be resurrected, and become like Gods, and reign in celestial kingdoms, principalities, and eternal dominions, while this cursed mob will sink to hell, the portion of all those who shed innocent blood.

"God has tried you. You are a good people; therefore I love you with all my heart. Greater love hath no man than that he should lay down his life for his friends. You have stood by me in the hour of trouble, and I am willing to sacrifice my life for your preservation.

"May the Lord God of Israel bless you forever and ever. I say it in the name of Jesus of Nazareth, and in the authority of the Holy Priesthood, which He hath conferred upon me."

The people said "Amen."

On the morning of June the 24th, 1844, Brother Joseph had an interview with the officers of the Legion, with the leading members of the City Council, and with the principal men of the city. The officers were instructed to dismiss their men, but to have them in a state of readiness to be called upon in any emergency that might occur.

About half past six o'clock the members of the City Council, the marshal, Brothers Joseph and Hyrum, and a number of others, started for Carthage on horseback."

On reaching the Temple, Joseph halted, and, looking admiringly upon it and upon the city, he said:

"This is the loveliest place and the best people under the heavens; little do they know the trials that await them."

He called on Brother Daniel H. Wells, who was sick, and not then a member of the Church. On parting with him he said:

"Squire Wells, I wish you to cherish my memory, and not think me the worst man in the world, either."

The same morning, after Hyrum had made ready to start, he read the following paragraph, near the close of the fifth chapter of Ether, in the Book of Mormon, and turned down the leaf upon it:

"And it came to pass that I prayed unto the Lord that he would give unto the Gentiles grace, that they might have charity. And it came to pass that the Lord said unto me, if they have not charity, it mattereth not unto you, thou hast been faithful; wherefore thy garments are clean. And because thou hast seen thy weakness, thou shalt be made strong, even unto the sitting down in the place which I have prepared in the mansions of my Father. And now I —— bid farewell unto the Gentiles; yea and also unto my brethren whom I love, until we shall meet before the judgment-seat of Christ, where all men shall know that my garments are not spotted with your blood."

Before reaching Carthage, they met Captain Dunn on his way to Nauvoo with an order from the governor for the "State arms." It was then that Joseph said, "*I am going like a lamb to the slaughter; but I am calm as a summer's morning; I have a conscience void of offense towards God, and towards all men; I shall die innocent.*"

When about to meet with this company Joseph said to the brethren:

"Do not be alarmed, brethren, for they cannot do more to you than the enemies of truth did to the ancient saints—they can only kill the body."

Joseph endorsed his acceptance on the governor's order for the arms, and returned with the posse to Nauvoo to obtain them; after which they turned back to Carthage, where they arrived a few minutes before twelve o'clock at night.

In the morning they had an interview with the governor and he pledged the faith of the State that they should be protected.

Joseph and Hyrum were then arrested on a charge of treason, upon a warrant founded on the oaths of H. O. Norton and Augustine Spencer.

The governor and General Demming afterwards conducted them before the McDonough County troops, an account of which is contained in the published history as follows:

"CARTHAGE, June 25th, 1844.

"Quarter past 9. The governor came and invited Joseph to walk with him through the troops. Joseph solicited a few moments' private conversation with him, which the governor refused.

"While refusing, the governor looked down at his shoes, as though he was ashamed. They then walked through the crowd, with Brigadier General Miner R. Demming, and Dr. Richards, to General Demming's quarters. The people appeared quiet until a company of Carthage Greys flocked round the doors of General Demming in an uproarious manner, of which notice was sent to the governor. In the meantime the governor had ordered the McDonough troops to be drawn up in line, for Joseph and Hyrum to pass in front of them, they having requested that they might have a clear view of the Generals Smith.

*Joseph had a conversation with the governor for about ten minutes, when he again pledged the faith of the State that he and his friends should be protected from violence.*

"Robinson, the postmaster, said, on report of martial law being proclaimed in Nauvoo, he had stopped the mail, and notified the post-master general of the state of things in Hancock County.

"From the general's quarters Joseph and Hyrum went in front of the lines, in a hollow square of a company of Carthage Greys. At seven minutes before ten they arrived in front of the lines, and passed before the whole, Joseph being on the right of General Demming and Hyrum on his left. Elders Richards, Taylor and Phelps following. Joseph and Hyrum were introduced by Governor Ford about twenty times along the line as General Joseph Smith and General Hyrum Smith, the governor walking in front on the left. The Carthage Greys refused to receive them by that introduction, and some of the officers threw up their hats, drew their swords, and said they would introduce themslves to the damned 'Mormons' in a different style. The governor mildly entreated them not to act so rudely, but their excitement increased; the governor, however, succeeded in pacifying them by making a speech, and promising them that they should have 'full satisfaction.'

"A little later a number of officers of the troops visited Joseph in his room. Joseph asked them if there was anything in his appearance that indicated that he was the desperate character that his enemies represented him to be; and he requested them to give him their honest opinion on the subject. The answer was:

"'No, sir, your appearance would indicate the very contrary, General Smith; but we cannot see what is in your heart, neither can we tell what are your intentions.'

"To which Joseph replied:

"'Very true, gentlemen, you cannot see what is in my heart, and you are therefore unable to judge me or my intentions; but I can see what is in your hearts, and will tell you what I see. I can see you thirst for blood, and nothing but my blood will satisfy you. It is not for crime of any description that I and my brethren are thus continually persecuted and harassed by our enemies, but there are other motives, and some of them I have expressed, so far as relates to myself; and inasmuch as you and the people thirst for blood, I prophesy, in the name of the Lord, that you shall witness scenes of blood and sorrow to your entire satisfaction. Your souls shall be perfectly satiated with blood, and many of you who are now present shall have an opportunity to face the cannon's mouth from sources you think not of; and those people that desire this great evil upon me and my brethren, shall be filled with regret and sorrow because of the scenes of desolation and distress that await them. They shall seek for peace, and shall not be able to find it. Gentlemen, you will find what I have told you to be true.'"

## CHAPTER VII.

COMMITED TO JAIL—MOB DESPAIR OF CONVICTING THE PRISONERS BY LEGAL PROCESS AND DETERMINE TO EFFECT THEIR PURPOSE BY POWDER AND BALL—GOVERNOR PROMISES TO TAKE THEM TO NAUVOO WITH HIM—SENDS MARSHAL GREENE TO NAUVOO TO KEEP ORDER DURING HIS VISIT—GOVERNOR FORD GOES TO NAUVOO, LEAVING THE PRISONERS TO THEIR FATE—A MOB WITH PAINTED FACES SURROUND THE JAIL AND MURDER JOSEPH AND HYRUM SMITH AND WOUND JOHN TAYLOR—NEWS OF THE MASSACRE SENT TO NAUVOO—GRIEF-STRICKEN COMMUNITY—ALARM OF THE MOBOCRATS—ARRIVAL OF THE BODIES OF THE MARTYRS.

The prisoners were committed to jail, June 25th. Soon after, some of the counsel for the prosecution expressed a wish that the prisoners should be brought out of jail for examination. Joseph's counsel remonstrated, saying: "The prisoners had already been committed, and that the justice and constable had no further control of them; and that if the prosecutors wished the prisoners brought out of jail, they should bring them out on a writ of *habeas corpus* or some other due course of law."

Notwithstanding this, the justice made out an order to the jailor which was given to a constable to execute, demanding that the bodies of Joseph and Hyrum Smith be brought forthwith from the jail, before him, for an examination on the charge of treason. The prisoners having been committed to the custody of the jailor until discharged by due course of law, and he knowing that the order was illegal, refused to deliver them to the constable; whereupon the governor's troops took them to the Court House, when the hearing was continued to the 29th, and they were returned to jail. It then began to be rumored, "*that there was nothing against these men; the law could not reach them, but powder and ball would!*"

It should be here stated that Joseph had on two or three occasions, since he arrived in Carthage, informed the governor that his life was not safe there, and if he (the governor) went to Nauvoo he wished to go along, so that he might have his protection. The governor gave him a promise, two or three times repeated, that in the event of his going to Nauvoo, he would take Joseph with him.

In conversation with the governor, Joseph said: "Furthermore, in relation to the press, you say that you differ with me in opinion. Be it so; the thing, after all, is only a legal difficulty, and the courts, I should judge, are competent to decide on that matter. If our act was illegal, we are willing to meet it."

But Joseph believed, that under the charter of the city of Nauvoo, the municipal court had the legal right to abate the *Expositor* as a nuisance. Still he acknowledged the jurisdiction of the higher courts, and if, upon investigation, the case should be decided against the city, he was ready to submit thereto and abide by it. He, in substance, so expressed himself to Governor Ford.

On the morning of June 27, 1844, John P. Greene, the City Marshal of Nauvoo, having been committed, in company with Joseph and Hyrum Smith, on a charge of treason, and confined in Carthage jail, was called out by the governor, and sent to Nauvoo to have the police on duty, and see that there were no riotous demonstrations on the part of the populace when he, the governor, should come into the city, he having concluded to visit Nauvoo that day. The marshal obtained a promise from the governor, before leaving, that he would bring Joseph and Hyrum Smith with him.

"The governor was made acquainted with the threats that had been made against the lives of the prisoners, but on the morning of the 27th, he disbanded the McDonough troops, and sent them home; took Captain Dunn's company of cavalry and proceeded to Nauvoo, leaving these two men and three or four friends, to be guarded by *eight men* at the jail; and a company in town of sixty men, eighty or one hundred rods from the jail, as a corps in reserve."

Says the *Times and Seasons*: "About six o'clock in the afternoon (June 27th) the guard was surprised by an armed mob of from one hundred and fifty to two hundred and fifty, painted red, black and yellow, which surrounded the jail, forced in—poured a shower of bullets into the room where these unfortunate men were held, 'in durance vile,' to answer to the laws of Illinois; under the solemn pledge of the faith of the State, by Governor Ford, *that they should be protected!* but the mob ruled!! They fell as martyrs amid this tornado of lead, each receiving four bullets! John Taylor was wounded by four bullets in his limbs. Thus perishes the hope of law; thus vanishes the plighted faith of the State; thus the blood of innocence stains the constituted authorities of the United States, and thus have two among the most noble martyrs since the slaughter of Abel, sealed the truth of their divine mission, by being shot by a mob for their religion."

While this bloody tragedy was being enacted at Carthage, Governor Ford, instead of protecting his prisoners as he had pledged his honor to do, was at Nauvoo. He stood upon the very frame of a building where Joseph, for the last time, had addressed the Legion, five or six days previously. He was speaking to a large assemblage of people, and, among other insulting things, gave utterance to the following:

"A great crime has been done by destroying the *Expositor* press and placing the city under martial law, and a *severe atonement must be made*, so prepare your minds for the emergency. Another cause of excitement is the fact of your having so many firearms; the public are afraid that you are going to use them to usurp the government. I know there is a great prejudice against you on account of your peculiar religion, but you ought to be praying Saints. not military Saints. Depend upon it, a little more misbehavior on the part of the citizens, and the torch which is now already lighted, will be applied; the city may be reduced to ashes, and extermination would inevitably follow; and it gave me great pain to think that there was danger of so many innocent women and children being exterminated. If anything of a serious character should befall the lives or property of the persons who are prosecuting your leaders, you will be held responsible."

News of the massacre was forthwith sent to Nauvoo, but the messengers did not arrive there until early next morning. They brought a letter signed by Willard Richards, John Taylor and Samuel H. Smith, stating that the governor had just arrived in Carthage, who stated that "all things shall be inquired into, and all right measures taken."

This letter contained the following items: "I say to all the citizens of Nauvoo, my brethren, be still, and know that *God reigns*. *Don't rush out of the city*—don't rush to Carthage; stay at home and be prepared for an attack from Missouri mobbers.

"We will prepare to move the bodies as soon as possible.

"The people of the County are greatly excited, and fear the 'Mormons' will come and take vengeance. I have pledged my word the 'Mormons' will stay at home as soon as they can be informed, and no violence will be used on their part."

To this letter is appended this note:

"Defend yourselves until protection can be furnished necessary. June 27th, 1844.

"THOMAS FORD,
"Governor and Commander in Chief."

And also the following:

"*Mr. Orson Spencer*,
"DEAR SIR:—Please deliberate on this matter; prudence may obviate material destruction. I was at my residence when this horrible crime was committed. It will be condemned by three-fourths of the citizens of the County—be quiet or you will be attacked from Missouri.

"M. R. DEMING."

The *Times and Seasons* further remarks:

"The governor as well as the citizens of Carthage, were thunderstruck! and fled.

"The Legion in Nauvoo was called out at ten a. m., and addressed by Judge Phelps, Colonel Buckmaster, of Alton, the governor's aid, and others; and all excitement and fury allayed, and preparations were made to receive the bodies of the noble martyrs. About three o'clock they were met by a great assemblage of people east of the Temple on Mulholland Street, under the direction of the City Marshal, followed by Samuel H. Smith, the brother of the deceased, Dr. Richards and Mr. Hamilton, of Carthage. The wagons were guarded by eight men. The procession that followed in Nauvoo, was the City Council, the Lieutenant-General's staff, Major-General and staff, the Brigadier General and staff, commanders and officers of the Legion and citizens generally, which numbered several thousands, amid the most solemn lamentations and wailings that ever ascended into the ears of the Lord of hosts to be avenged of our enemies.

"When the procession arrived, the bodies were both taken into the Nauvoo Mansion. The scene at the Mansion cannot be described. The audience was addressed by Dr. Richards, Judge Phelps, Woods and Reed, Esquires, of Iowa, and Colonel Markham. It was a vast assemblage of some eight or ten thousand persons, and with one united voice they resolved to trust to the law for a remedy of such a high-handed assassination, and when that failed, to call upon God to avenge them of their wrongs! Oh! widows and orphans! Oh! Americans weep! for the glory of freedom has departed!"

After the bodies of the honored dead were dressed and fully prepared, they were placed in coffins and lay in state, in the large dining room, where many thousands of people passed through, two by two, and viewed, for the last time, their earthly remains.

That scene was one of great solemnity. Language is too feeble to draw an adequate picture. The deep and pungent emotions that are ingenerate in the bosom, cannot be declared in words, when thus stirred to their inmost depths. The lacerated heart must feel the extent of its own woes, and with that be content. Words are far too impotent to transmit it to the full understanding of another.

Death, in any form, is an unwelcome visitant, and casts a shadow over us, that oppresses with its gloominess. But when the good, the generous, the philanthopist, the towering patriot and champion of equal rights, is cut down in the prime of manhood and in the midst of usefulness, by a ruthless hand, then, indeed, is the grief intensified and made uncontrollable, even to the most philosophic mind.

These were the devoted leaders of a great people. They were the favored of heaven, the commissioned of the Great Eternal One. They were the chosen delegates to move the cause of righteousness among the nations, preparatory to the coming of the Son of Man. They testified of peace and good-will, but the fury of the wicked encompassed them with the tempest of passion, and Carthage prison and the State escutcheon were crimsoned with their innocent blood.

They had been humble and patient, yet persevering in pushing forward their mission of love. Through perils they had passed undismayed. The menace of mobs could not awe them into silence. In prison they stood erect in dignity, as a tyrant's chains hung upon them. They loved their country's laws because, if properly executed, they were calculated to shelter the honest sons of toil under the shadow of the tree of liberty.

High-minded and honorable, yet kind and gentle in deportment, they won the love, esteem and confidence of all who knew them best. To them the widow and fatherless looked for encouragement, and the down-trodden and oppressed turned to them for protection.

But, alas! the tragedy had been enacted! Assassination had fired the deadly volley and their perforated forms lay motionless in the embrace of death. It was so. Words are useless now.

## CHAPTER VIII.

ACCOUNT OF THE MASSACRE BY ONE WHO WAS AMONG THE MOB—PROBABLE FATE OF THIS IMFORMER—HOW HE HAPPENED TO BE WITH THE MOB PARTY—DETAILS OF THE MASSACRE—REFLECTIONS ON THE HORRIBLE DEED—RETURN TO HIS HOME—A DREAM—DETERMINATION TO DO WHAT HE COULD TO BRING THE MURDERERS TO JUSTICE—VISIT TO NAUVOO AND QUINCY—HUSH-MONEY OFFERED HIM—HE JOINS THE CHURCH—EFFORTS TO PUT HIM OUT OF THE WAY—BEFORE THE GRAND JURY AS A WITNESS—NINE PERSONS INDICTED—MURDERERS ALLOWED TO GO FREE.

MANY of the facts connected with the murder of Joseph and Hyrum Smith have now been related. But the questions arise: Who committed the deed? In what manner was it accomplished?

To fully present this phase of the cruel butchery, the following statements of an eye-witness are introduced. It is an account given by Wm. M. Daniels, which was written out carefully by the author of this volume, and printed in a pamphlet, at Nauvoo.

Mr. Daniels, for some time after the murder, resided in Nauvoo, where he joined the Church. In justice to him it should be here stated that he evinced the fullest sincerity while relating the incidents of his narrative. As regards the flash of light described by him, which is illustrated in our engraving, he averred most emphatically that it occurred as related. Even before the court, when the murderers were arraigned for examination as to their complicity in the bloody deed, he was confronted by the lawyers for the mob party, and there stated that all he had told was the truth.

As to the correctness of this strange exhibition of light, the author knows nothing personally; but it is given as Daniels' testimony, among the other incidents, and he leaves the reader to draw such conclusions as may seem reasonable.

The whereabouts of Mr. Daniels has been unknown to the writer since 1846. It is not at all unlikely that some of the parties implicated in the tragedy at Carthage assassinated him for exposing them. They swore they would do so, and were hunting for him previous to the exodus of the Saints from Nauvoo. On the steamboat *Ocean Wave* a party of them tried to get some information, as to where Daniels might be found, from, and also laid a cunning plan to entrap, the writer when the boat should land at Warsaw, for the part he took in the publication—but they failed.

The following is the statement of Daniels:

I resided in Augusta, Hancock County, Ill., eighteen miles from Carthage. On the 16th day of June, I left my home with the intention of going to St. Louis. When I arrived at Bear Creek, I found the country in a great state of excitement, in relation to the "Mormons." I was told it would be dangerous for me to proceed farther on my way to Warsaw, as the intermediate country was mostly settled by "Mormons," who would, in all probability, intercept me by violence. I knew nothing of the character and disposition of the "Mormon" people, never having been personally acquainted with them as a community,

The tales of villainy that were related concerning them, were so horrid and shocking that I yielded to the entreaties of my advisers, and abandoned, for that day, at least, my intention of proceeding farther on my journey. I lodged that night with a Mr. Scott.

The next morning a company of men were going from that place to Carthage, for the purpose, as they said, of assisting the militia to drive the "Mormons" out of the country. Out of curiosity, as I had no particular way to spend my time, and the creeks having been rendered impassable that night by heavy rain, I went in company with them to Carthage. On our way there, they were discussing the best means to be adopted for the expulsion of the "Mormon" population. Some were for marching to Nauvoo, and laying the city in ashes, and driving the inhabitants from the limits of the State, at the point of the bayonet; others were for murdering Joseph and Hyrum Smith, while others were in favor of accomplishing both of these barbarous objects.

I noticed minutely their conversation, and it was not hard for me to discover that all their animosity and hatred of their neighbors, arose from a spirit of envy. I heard no person declaring that the "Mormons" had ever personally injured him; but they swore that "Old Joe" was getting too much power and influence in the world, and he ought to be put out of the way. His career ought to be stopped. They looked upon him as no less than a second Mahomet, who would soon spring into power, usurp the reins of government, and establish his religion by the sword. To prevent such a calamity from befalling the world, they argued that it would be doing God service to take his life, supposing that would also totally annihilate the religion called "Mormonism."

From that hour I looked upon them as demons, not men, and determined to do all in my power to prevent so bloody and awful an occurrence. I was not attached to any religious society whatever, and was willing that all mankind should worship Almighty God according to the dictates of their own consciences. I knew that the laws of my country, which I had been taught to honor and revere, granted all men that right and privilege, while they were the subjects of its government. I hoped that her institutions might be untarnished and her dignity unsullied and free from so disgraceful an event as was then in contemplation.

We arrived in Carthage, and found the Carthage Greys, and several other companies, on parade. I was told their object was to drive the "Mormons." I would remark that a certain preacher, professing to be a minister of the gospel of Jesus Christ to the world, was engaged in playing a drum at the head of this company.

## INFLAMMATORY SPEECHES ABOUT THE "MORMONS." 73

These companies were commanded by Captains Smith, Green and others, who were greatly excited, and said they were determined to kill the "Mormons." On hearing that the governor was on his way to Carthage, they were very much alarmed; whereupon Joseph H. Jackson, in company with Dr. Foster, F. M. Higbee, and others, declared that if the Governor, "Tom" Ford, came, and gave the Smiths—Joseph and Hyrum—a fair trial, they would be acquitted, and we will be hung as sure as there is a God in heaven. Further he observed, "I do not see why the d——d little governor could not stay at home, and send us word, and we would do the business up in a hurry, and drive the 'Mormons' out of the country."

I returned to Bear Creek that night, with the intention of leaving for St. Louis the next morning. However, on the morning of the 20th, hearing that the Governor had arrived at Carthage, and being somewhat acquainted with him, I concluded to return and see him, which I did.

When I arrived at Carthage, he was addressing the people at the Court House, in relation to the "Mormon" difficulties. He said he came there to see that the law was fully carried out. When he was done, Mr. Roosevelt, of Warsaw, went upon the public square, mounted a box, and made an inflammatory speech to the people who had collected, wherein he stated that the law was not sufficient to carry out their measures. Stretching out his arms at full length, he said, with all the energy in his power: *"We have the willing minds, and God Almighty has given us strength, and we will wield the sabre and make our own laws!!"* He then said he presumed that the governor meant well enough, but was too easy in his remarks to them, in saying that he wished a compliance with the laws.

Mr. Roosevelt soon gave way for Mr. Skinner, a "young limb of the law," a tool for mobocracy, and, at the time, a candidate for the Legislature, who made a short speech, wherein he stated he was one of the delegates appointed by the people of Carthage to go to Springfield and lay before the governor their grievances. He was not so severe upon the governor as Mr. Roosevelt had been. He presumed the governor would do what was right, but his ultimate course proved him to be the most hypocritical.

The governor gave orders, which were read by Capt. Dunn, that all the people who had been promiscuously assembled in Carthage, should be consolidated in the militia, under his command, to co-operative in maintaining the supremacy of the law.

I returned to Bear Creek that evening. In the morning, I proceeded to Warsaw. On my arrival there, a force of about three hundred men was mustered upon the parade ground under the command of Captains Aldrich Grover, Elliott, and Col. Williams of Green Plains. I wished to know what their intentions were, and was informed that they were determined to drive the d——d Mormons out of the County. I remained there five days; during which time Williams, Roosevelt, Sharp, and others, were continually beating up for volunteers, by making inflammatory speeches, exciting the populace and making false publications to the world. Col Williams announced that he was empowered by the governor, to stop and search steamboats, at the wharf, at Warsaw. Accordingly, he stopped the steam packet *Osprey*. On Capt. Anderson's refusal to let him search the boat, he ordered his men to fire upon her. The cannon was leveled upon the boat. As they were in the act of firing, a gentlemen who was standing by, being sober, (for most of them were badly intoxicated) placed his hand between the match and powder, which prevented ignition. They, however, searched the boat; but did not succeed in finding but eight or nine kegs of powder, which they permitted to remain on board. That evening they fired upon two more steamboats, with their muskets, which they compelled to stop. Col Williams informed the Captains, that he had orders to search their boats for ammunition, arms, provisions, etc. The captains consented, and search was instituted, but nothing was found which was considered contraband, and the boats resumed their course.

Relative to the governor's giving the people of Warsaw orders to stop and search steamboats, I would remark that Gov. Ford informed me at Quincy, that he had not given them orders to stop any boats, with the exception of the *Maid of Iowa*, a boat then owned by the "Mormons," which the people supposed might convey away Gen. Smith. Here we see a willful and arbitrary infraction of law and order, on the part of this military Nero, Col. Williams, and the mobbers of Warsaw.

All was commotion and turmoil through Warsaw and its vicinity. The scenery had become insipid and irksome to me, and I longed for relief and to be where my mind could be at rest. Passing through such continual bustle, watching the movements of the rabble who, like a horde of impetuous barbarians, seemed impelled on, by the blind infatuation of priests and shallow zealots, in hopes of booty, disgusted and sickened me and fired me with contempt. My mind reverted to the time when the dark and bloody Attila led on the ignorant Huns to conquest, plunder and extermination, applying the torch of conflagration to pleasant villages and sequestered homes.

On Tuesday, I started for Quincy. As I pursued my journey from Warsaw, my mind was uneasy and restless. When I had travelled near eight miles I enquired my way, and, through accident or design, I was placed upon a road that led me directly back to Warsaw. My mind was composed and tranquil as I came in sight of the place. My attention was attracted by a group of men, apparently in earnest conversation. I drew near and learned that the Carthage Greys had made them the proposition to come to Carthage, on the following day, and assist them in murdering Joseph and Hyrum Smith, during the absence of the governor, at Golden's Point, where he contemplated marching with the troops. As soon as they discovered that I had learned the purpose of their conference, they became suspicious of me, fearing exposure, no doubt, and put me under guard. I was held in custody until the following morning, when a company of volunteers was raised, to march to Golden's Point, to unite with the governor. I desired to make the governor acquainted with what was contemplated against the lives of the prisoners. To effect this object, I volunteered, and drew a musket. The company was paraded in single file; roll was called and Capt. Jacob Davis, (the murderer, who was afterward screened from justice by the Senate of Illinois,) and Capt. Grover, selected ten men each from their respective companies, who were to march to Carthage, in compliance with the request of the Carthage Greys, to co-operative with them in committing the murder. These twenty men were marched a short distance to one side. where they received their instructions from Col. Williams, Mark Aldrich, Capt. Jacob Davis, and Capt. Grover, and they were sent off. I do not recollect the names of any of these twenty, with the exception of two brothers—coopers in Warsaw, by the name of Stevens. One of them is about six feet three inches high, well proportioned and athletic. The other is near five feet nine inches high, with dark complexion and dark hair. When the officers were interrogated as to the object of these twenty men being sent in advance of the troops, they evaded the truth by replying that they had been detailed for a picket guard.

The troops were marched. We arrived at the crossing of the railroad at 12 o'clock. We were there met by Sharp and others, bearing dispatches from the governor, disbanding the troops. This unexpected order threw the troops into a perfect panic. They cursed the governor for not permitting them to march through to Nauvoo. Their object in wishing to go—and this was understood with all the militia—was to burn the city and exterminate the inhabitants. These designs were baffled by the disbanding of the troops. In justice to the character of Governor Ford, I would remark that his object in disbanding the troops, was to prevent such an awful calamity.

The disbanding orders were read by Col. Levi Williams. Captains Davis, Grover and Elliott, immediately called their companies together.

Thomas C. Sharp mounted his "big bay horse," and made an inflammatory speech to the companies, characteristic of his corrupt heart. The following is a short extract, as near as my memory will serve me:

"FRIENDS AND FELLOW-CITIZENS! The crisis has arrived when it becomes our duty to rise, as freemen, and assert our rights. The law is insufficient for us; the governor will not enforce it; we must take it into our hands; we know what wrongs we suffer, and we are the best calculated to redress them. Now is the time to put a period to the mad career of the Prophet; sustained as he is by a band of fanatical military saints! We have borne his usurpations until it would be cowardice to bear them longer! My Fellow citizens! improve the opportunity that offers; lest the opportunity pass, and the despotic Prophet will never again be in your power. All things are understood, we must hasten to Carthage and murder the Smiths, while the governor is absent at Nauvoo. Beard the lions in their den. The news will reach Nauvoo before the governor leaves. This will so enrage the "Mormons," that they will fall upon and murder Tom Ford, and we shall then be rid of the d——d little governor and the 'Mormons' too." (Cheers.)

This speech was likely to fail of having the desired effect. None seemed willing to be the first to start. At last Capt. Grover started, and declared he would go alone, if no person would follow him. Soon one person followed, then another, until a company of eighty-four was made up. All the troops that had not volunteered in this company were told to go home. The twenty men who had been sent forward to commit the murder, were sent for and they formed a part of the eighty-four.

Here I felt that the purpose for which I volunteered, had been baffled. I expected to have met with the governor at Golden's Point, and could I have done so, I entertained no doubt, I could have succeeded in putting a stop to the murder. But instead of marching to Golden's Point as we anticipated, he marched to Nauvoo. Under these circumstances I was at a loss to know what to do. I had not time to go to Nauvoo, and raise a *posse* to surround the jail as a guard, before this company would arrive there. I was on foot, and would have ten or twelve miles farther to travel than they. As I could do nothing better, I was determined to follow on with the company and see what they would do. Several others, like myself, followed out of curiosity, without being armed. Carthage lay directly on my route home.

After we had arrived within nearly six miles of Carthage, they made a halt. Col. Williams rode three or four times backwards and forwards from the company to the Carthage Greys. He said he would have the Carthage Greys come and meet them. They marched within four miles of Carthage, when they were met by one of the Greys, bringing a note to the following import:

"Now is a delightful time to murder the Smiths. The governor has gone to Nauvoo with all the troops. The Carthage

Greys are left to guard the prisoners. Five of our men will be stationed at the jail; the rest will be upon the public square. To keep up appearances, you will attack the men at the jail—a sham scuffle will ensue—their guns will be loaded with blank cartridges—they will fire in the air."

They were also instructed by the person bearing this dispatch, to fire three guns as they advanced along the fence that led from the woods to the jail. This was to serve as a signal to the Carthage Greys, that they were in readiness.

After they had received their instructions, the company followed along up the hollow that struck into the point of timber.

Here I left them, and pursued my way to the jail, where I arrived ten or fifteen minutes first. How gladly would I have informed the defenseless prisoners of the plot that was shortly to be executed against them. Had the Carthage Greys been loyal members of the militia of the country, I could have effected their escape; but it was impossible.

Soon the mob made their appearance. They advanced in single file along the fence, as they had been instructed. When they had gained about half the distance of the fence, the signal guns were fired.

Soon the jail was surrounded by the mob. They had blacked themselves with wet powder, while they were in the woods, which gave them the horrible appearance of demons. The most of them had on blue hunting-shirts, with fringe around the edges.

The Carthage Greys advanced within about eight rods of the jail where they halted, in plain view of the whole transaction, until the deed was executed. They occupied a place in an eastern direction from the jail. When they halted, their commander, Capt. Smith, marched in front of the mob, said "How do you do, gentlemen?" and passed through their ranks, taking a station in their rear.

Col. Williams shouted out, "Rush in!—there's no danger boys—all is right!"

A sham rencounter ensued between them and the guard. They clinched each other, and the mob threw some of them upon the ground. A few guns were fired in the air.

A rush was made in the door, at the south part of the building. This let them into a hall, or entry, from which they ascended a flight of stairs, at the head of which, turning to the right, they reached the door that led into the prisoners' room.

To give a relation of some of the particular circumstances that transpired in the jail, I am compelled to depend, principally, upon the statements of others. My sources of information, upon these points, however, are of such a nature that the reader can regard them as strictly correct.

The spirits of the prisoners had been rather depressed all the afternoon. Why it was so they knew not. They knew the faith of the governor, and the State of Illinois, was pledged for their protection. Elder John Taylor had been singing a hymn, found on the 254th page of the English edition of the Latter-day Saints' Hymn Book, entitled, "A Poor Wayfaring Man of Grief."

This seemed rather applicable to their situation; it had a solemnity in it that tranqualized their minds, and at the request of Hyrum Smith, it was sung over again.

From this pleasant communion, they were aroused by curses, threats, and the heavy and fierce rush of the mob up the stairs.

Hyrum stood near the center of the room, in front of the door. The mob fired a ball through the pannel of the door, which entered Hyrum's head, at the left side of his nose. He fell upon his back, with his head one or two feet from the north east corner of the room, exclaiming, as he fell, "I am a dead man!" In all, four balls entered his body. One ball (it must have been fired through the window, from the outside) passed through his body with such force—entering his back—that it completely broke to pieces a watch which he wore in his vest pocket.

His death was sudden and without pain. Thus fell Hyrum Smith, the Patriarch of the Church of God, a martyr for his holy religion! In that brief moment was the Church of Jesus Christ deprived of the services of as good a man as ever had a name in its history.

A shower of balls were poured through all parts of the room, many of which lodged in the ceiling, just above the head of the fallen man.

A few hours previous to this, a friend to General Joseph Smith, put in his possession a revolving pistol with six chambers, usually called a "pepper-box." With this in his hand, he took a position by the wall at the left of the door.

Joseph reached his pistol through the door, which was pushed a little ajar, and fired three of the barrels; the rest missed fire. He wounded three of the assailants—two mortally—one of whom, as he rushed down out of the door, was asked if he was badly hurt. He replied, "Yes; my arm is shot all to pieces by Old Joe; but I don't care, I've got reveng; I shot Hyrum!"

Elder Taylor took a position beside the door, with Elder Richards, and parried off their muskets with walking sticks, as they were firing.

What must have been the feelings of General Smith, at this critical juncture! He had fired all of the barrels of his pistol that would discharge; he had therefore no further means of defense. His brother, whose life he had been so anxious to preserve, lay a corpse before him, and his assailants were filling the door with muskets and firing showers of lead into the room.

Elder Taylor continued parrying their guns, until they had got them about half the length into the room, when he found resistance vain and attempted to jump out of the window. Just then a ball from within struck him on the left thigh; hitting the bone, it glanced through to within half an inch of the other side. He fell on the window-sill and expected he would fall out, when a ball from without struck his watch, which he carried in his vest pocket, and threw him back into the room. He was hit by two more balls; one injuring his left wrist considerably, and the other entering at the side of the bone, just below the left knee. He fell into the room, and rolled under a bed that stood at the right of the window, in the south-east corner of the room. While under the bed, he was fired at several times, and was struck by one ball which tore the flesh on his left hip in a shocking manner, throwing large quantities of blood upon the wall and floor. These wounds proved very severe and painful, but he suffered without a murmur, rejoicing that he had the satisfaction to mingle his blood with that of the Prophets, and be with them in the last moments of their earthly existence. His blood, with theirs, can cry to heaven for vengeance on those who have shed the blood of innocence and slain the servants of the living God in all ages of the world. This seemed a source of high gratification, and he endured his severe sufferings without a single complaint, being perfectly resigned to the providence of God.

Elder Richards was still contending with the assailants, at the door, when General Smith, seeing there was no safety in the room, and probably thinking it might save the lives of others if he could escape from the room, turned calmly from the door, dropped his pistol upon the floor, saying, "There, defend yourselves as well as you can."

He sprang into the window; but just as he was preparing to descend, he saw such an array of bayonets below, that he caught by the window casing, where he hung by his hands and feet, with his head to the north, feet to the south, and his body swinging downwards. He hung in that position three or four minutes, during which time he exclaimed, two or three times, "O, LORD, MY GOD!!!" and fell to the ground. While he was hanging in that position, Col. Williams hallooed, "Shoot him! G—d d—n him! shoot the dam'd rascal!" However, none fired at him.

He seemed to fall easy. He struck partly on his right shoulder and back, his neck and head reaching the ground a little before his feet. He rolled instantly on his face. From this position he was taken by a young man, who sprang to him from the other side of the fence, who held a pewter fife in his hand, was barefoot and bare-headed, having on no coat, with his pants rolled above his knees, and shirt-sleeves above his elbows. He set President Smith against the south side of the well-curb, that was situated a few feet from the jail. While doing this, the savage muttered aloud, "This is Old Jo; I know him. I know you, Old Jo. Damn you; you are the man that had my daddy shot." The object he had in talking in this way, I supposed to be this: He wished to have President Smith and the people in general, believe he was the son of Governor Boggs, which would lead to the opinion that it was the Missourians who had come over and committed the murder. This was the report that they soon caused to be circulated; but this was too palpable an absurdity to be credited.

After President Smith had fallen, I saw Elder Willard Richards come to the window and look out upon the horrid scene that spread itself below him.

I could not help noticing the striking contrast in the countenance of President Smith and the horrid, demon-like appearance of his murderers. The former was calm and tranquil, while the mob were filled with excitement and agitation.

President Smith's exit from the room had the tendency to cause those who were firing into the room to abandon it and rush to the outside. This gave an opportunity for Elder Richards to convey Elder Taylor into the cell, which he did, and covered him with a bed, thinking he might there be secure if the mob should make another rush into the jail. While they were in the cell, some of the mob again entered the room; but finding it deserted by all but Hyrum Smith, they left the jail. (See engraving.)

When President Smith had been set against the curb, and began to recover, from the effects of the fall, Col. Williams ordered four men to shoot him. Accordingly, four men took an eastern direction, about eight feet from the curb, Col. Williams standing partly at their rear, and made ready to execute the order. While they were making preparations, and the muskets were raised to their faces, President Smith's eyes rested upon them with a calm and quiet resignation. He betrayed no agitated feelings and the expression upon his countenance seemed to betoken his inly prayer to be. "O, Father, forgive them, for they know not what they do."

"The fire was simultaneous. A slight cringe of the body was all the indication of pain that he betrayed when the balls struck him. He fell upon his face. One ball then entered the back part of his body. This is the ball that many people have supposed struck him about the time he was in the window. But

this is a mistake. I was close by him, and I know he was not hit with a ball, until after he was seated by the well-curb.

His death was instantaneous and tranquil. He betrayed no appearance of pain. His noble form exhibited all its powers of manly strength and healthful agility, yet not a muscle seemed to move with pain, and there was no distortion of his features. His death was peaceful as the falling to sleep of an infant—no cloud of contending passion gathered upon his brow, and no malediction trembled on his lip. The reward of a righteous man seemed hovering over him, and his breath ceased with as much ease and gentleness, as if eternity was exerting an influence in his behalf and taking his spirit home to a world of "liberty, light and life."

The ruffian, of whom I have spoken, who set him against the well-curb, now secured a bowie knife for the purpose of severing his head from his body. He raised the knife and was in the attitude of striking, when a light, so sudden and powerful, burst from the heavens upon the bloody scene, (passing its vivid chain between Joseph and his murderers,) that they were struck with terrified awe and filled with consternation. This light, in its appearance and potency, baffles all powers of description. The arm of the ruffian, that held the knife, fell powerless; the muskets of the four, who fired, fell to the ground, and they all stood like marble statues, not having power to move a single limb of their bodies.

By this time most of the men had fled in great disorder. I never saw so frightened a set of men before. Col. Williams saw the light and was also badly frightened; but he did not entirely lose the use of his limbs or speech. Seeing the condition of these men, he hallooed to some who had just commenced to retreat, for God's sake to come and carry off these men. They came back and carried them by main strength towards the baggage wagons. They seemed as helpless as if they were dead.

The storm had passed away. The cowardly demons had fled, and I stood a spectator, gazing on the scene. There lay Joseph Smith, the martyred leader of thousands who revered him. The man who had passed like a magic spirit through society, and in a career of a few years, had lit up the world with wonder, astonishment and admiration, was left dead upon the ground! He lay full low; yet, in my contemplations, I regarded him as the triumphant conqueror left master of the bloody field. Eighty-four men, (fiends,) armed with United States' muskets and other weapons, had the unparalleled heroism to murder him while a prisoner; (!!) while he had the nerve and presence of mind to contend with such unequal force, and with a pocket pistol kill and wound as many as they. In him was the spirit of dauntless bravery exemplified.

But a few days before his noble figure rode at the head of a mighty legion, numbering five thousand brave hearts and ten thousand strong arms. His presence gave them courage, his words animated their hearts and nerved their limbs; and the large heart that beat within his manly breast, entwined around it their love and affection, by the generosity and nobility of its principles.

In this situation he had the power to defend himself. How insignificant was the power of this contemptible mob, in comparison with this force, that could have borne him off triumphant, in defiance of all their resistance! From this position of power he descended—threw down the sword that could have protected him from the menace of mobs—and trusted himself to the honor and fidelity of men and the boasted majesty of American jurisprudence!

O, man! how worthless are your promises! how perfidious are your ways! He that would have died for the maintenance of his honor, fell a sacrifice to the broken faith of other men!

The murder took place at fifteen minutes past five o'clock, p. m., June 27, 1844.

I now determined to go to my home. As I passed through the streets of Carthage, I found that the feeling of consternation had seized upon the hearts of its citizens and spread throughout its vicinity. The inhabitants, men and women, were running in every direction through the streets; some flying in wagons, and others on foot, to the country, and others preparing for flight. They entertained no other idea but that the "Mormons" would be upon them and desolate their neighborhoods, from one extremity of the County to the other. They knew they had committed a deed that would have justified them in taking summary vengeance; they felt that they deserved it and their conscience told them they might expect it. But the course taken by the people of Nauvoo, so entirely different from this, is known to all. I cannot believe there is another people on earth, who could have remained within the boundary of a city, and had two of their leading citizens murdered, under the same circumstances, without breaking over all restraint and wreaking vengeance upon the lawless rabble who had thus tampered with their reposed confidence. "Vengeance is mine, saith the Lord, and I will repay."

In a few hours, Carthage was desolate, and seemed the sight of some dilapidated village, whose inhabitants had long since mingled their dust in the general ruin. I might have imagined myself among the relics of some fallen metropolis; but the emotions of my bosom were already too keen for me to court the reflections of loneliness, and I hastened from the scene to calm my feelings amid the consolations of home.

## A DREAM.

When I enjoyed the smiling welcome of a wife, I asked my heart if aught I had done had contributed to make wives widows and children orphans. A conscience void of offense told me I was guiltless. Yet I was restless and uneasy. Through the reflections of the joyless day and the vigils of the sleepless night, the quick rush of the demons upon the jail—the roar of musketry—Joseph falling from the window—his countenance calm, and his bosom soothed in the quiet hush of oblivion—the grim visages of the mob, damnable as the spirits of hell—and the mysterious light, that came like a paralytic shock over the murderers—passed in regular succession through my mind, and rest and sleep, withheld from me their necessary comforts. Time passed in this way until the third night after the murder, when a pleasant dream brought back that contentment and quietude that I was wont to enjoy. This is a relation of my dream:

Joseph stood before me. A smile of approbation was upon his cheek and his eyes rested upon me pleasantly, beaming with the bright warm tokens of friendship. It was then manifested to me that all I had done was approved of him and God. He took me up into a high mountain. While toiling up its side, I would frequently slip back and occasionally sink my feet into its side, which was rendered soft by the dampness of the soil. Whenever this occurred, Joseph would reach out his hand and help me along. In this way, we finally reached the summit, which presented a broad scope of table land. Here I was seated. Joseph gave me a glass of clear cold water. He then placed his hands upon my head, prayed to the Lord, blessed me and departed.

This dream had an effect upon my mind that was irresistible and determined my future course. I resolved to do all in my power for the vindication of innocence and the punishment of crime. In determining upon this course, I saw no prospect before me but to have my life hunted by night and by day. It was plunging my family into a life of anxiety and deprivation; yet I was determined to pass through it all, regardless of consequences. I knew what to expect if I turned informer, for while we were on our way from the crossing of the railroad to Carthage, one of the miscreants took pains, very insinuatingly, to inform me that if any person informed on them he would be put out of the way.

The next morning I went to see a friend of mine, and told him all I had witnessed. He advised me to go immediately to the leading men of Nauvoo. I did so, taking from him letters of introduction. On presenting my letter to Elder Richards, and informing him of the nature of my business, he informed me that my knowledge would be of no particular use to them, as they should wait for the proper officers of the State to move forward in the matter. However, I deemed it compatible with duty to make affidavit of the facts, which I did by going before Esquire Johnson.

From there, I went to Quincy, where I met with Governor Ford. He thanked me for the information I gave him, and said my testimony would be required, as measures would be adopted to bring the murderers to justice.

I now desired to return home; but knowing that my life would not be safe in Hancock County, I concluded to send for my family and remain in Quincy.

The mob party, learning that I was a witness against them, resorted to many stratagems to get me to leave the country. Among these, there was one that I wish to mention. One day I was met by a couple of men who told me if I would leave the country, and not appear against the murderers, they would pay me twenty-five hundred dollars. I, of course, refused. They shook the money at me, no doubt, thinking to tempt me and make me forget my duty. Scorning the acceptance of their accursed gold, I told them I had not time to talk with them, and, turning on my heel, walked away. I mention this to show the black-hearted villainy of the murderers that composed the society of Warsaw and Carthage. It is a fact that a majority of the inhabitants of each of these places, were either engaged in the murder, or sanctioned it in their hearts or by their actions. When have they lifted their voices and protested against any participation in the damnable deed? When have they declared that their garments are pure from the blood that sticks, like a curse, to the walls and floor of their County jail? When have they ever "crooked a finger" towards the commitment of those devils whose bloody act should have stamped them with eternal infamy in the eyes of the people of these places? Is there not found upon them a sprinkling of that blood, which shall be like a consuming moth upon them?

I now yielded obedience to the gospel of Jesus Christ, the truth of which I had seen sealed by the blood of the Prophets, who had been the honored instruments made use of in the hands of God, of revealing it in the last days to the children of men. I here bear record of its truth, and testify that I verily know Joseph Smith was a servant of the living God. The evidence I received at his martyrdom, in seeing the heavens exert a power for the protection of his body, is, to me, plain and irresistible.

It is well known that there was a large reward offered, by the Missourians for the head of General Smith, and probably it was to get this reward that the ruffian was about to sever his head from his body. But although God suffered them to take his life, He would not suffer them to mangle his body and effect this wicked purpose. Hence this exhibition of His power.

The 27th of September was the time set by the people of Hancock to carry into execution the much talked of wolf hunt.* Satisfactory information coming to the ears of the governor, that the design was to hunt something besides prairie wolves, and being warned by the transactions of the 27th of June, he ordered out a sufficient force of the militia of the State, and marched, in person, to the seat of contemplated aggression. His appearance there greatly chagrined the mobocrats of the County, who had not sufficiently glutted themselves with innocent blood. Thus a termination was put to further general hostilities, for a time at least. From there he marched to Quincy, where I had another interview with him. He declared his determination to have justice done, and charged me in the name of God not to leave the State.

Previous to the session of the circuit court at Carthage, I was subpœnaed to appear on behalf of the State. When the time arrived, I proceeded about twenty-two miles alone. I deemed it unsafe to go farther without a guard, and seventeen of my friends volunteered to accompany me to Nauvoo. I had left Mr. Fellows', four miles west of Carthage, a short time, when eleven men, all armed, rode up in a wagon and halted a short distance from Mr. Fellows' house. They passed, four at a time, backwards and forwards before the door, looking into the door and windows as they passed along. One or two gentlemen went out and interrogated them as to their business; but no satisfactory answer could be extorted. They kept things very sly; yet their purpose has been made known to me. They did not find the person for whose blood they thirsted. I arrived in safety at Nauvoo.

The next night I was awakened by the sheriff. He had come after me, deeming it unsafe for me to travel in the daytime. We arrived in Carthage early in the morning, and about nine o'clock I was called into the grand jury room. My appearance in Carthage created considerable sensation in the breasts of mobbers; but I went in regardless of every show of hostility. While giving in my testimony, several of the mob armed themselves and left the town, no doubt for the purpose of waylaying me, expecting I would return after dark. I thought it most prudent to leave immediately, which I did, and succeeded in arriving in safety again at Nauvoo.

Nine persons were indicted by the grand jury, for the murder, to wit: *Honorable* (?) Jacob C. Davis, Colonel

*——On the pretense of engaging in a general wolf-hunt, preparations were made by the mobocrats to raid upon the settlements of the Saints and massacre the inhabitants.

Levi Williams, Thomas C. Sharp, William N. Grover, Mark Aldrich, William Voris, Goliher, Allen and Wills.

What has been the course pursued with these persons? Have they been confined in jail, as criminals commonly are after indictment? No. Jacob C. Davis has since filled his seat in the senate of Illinois; Thomas C. Sharp has since been upheld and patronized as an editor; and the remainder of them have enjoyed all the privileges of citizens who never committed crime!

Not one solitary person has ever seen the inside wall of a jail for that murder, with the exception of John C. Elliot, who was arrested and examined in Nauvoo, and committed for trial before the circuit court; and he remained in jail only a very short time.

People talk about "Mormon" thieves, when they have eighty-four beings, fiends in human shape, running at large in their community, who were actually engaged in murder! The people of Illinois talk about "Mormon" usurpation, and treasonable designs in their leaders, and their senate chamber echoing with the denunciations of a fiend yet dripping with the warm blood of innocence! The legislature and governor repeal the Nauvoo City charter, for some pretended stretch of municipal power, and they welcome to their councils a being with an indictment hanging over his head for the highest crime known to the laws! They talk about the "Mormon" abuse of the *habeas corpus*, while they pass special decrees that no member shall be subject to any process, whether civil or criminal, during the session of the senate, for the special benefit of a murderer, thereby releasing him from the custody of the sheriff, and screening him from justice! They prate about "Mormon" disloyalty, while the plighted faith of the State is broken, and her honor trampled in the dust!

Gentle reader, I have given as faithful a narrative as I possibly could. I have related scenes through which I have passed myself—scenes of danger, excitement and wickedness. My life has been hunted by day and by night; the quietude of my family has been broken up, and the villains are still determined to take my life. I have thus far eluded them; but I know not when my life may be taken as a sacrifice, to atone for telling the truth in a *free* country. But I am at the defiance of devils and emissaries of hell, and will not shrink from duty, or cower under their menaces.

## CHAPTER IX.

LETTER FROM THE MAN WHO ATTEMPTED TO CUT JOSEPH SMITH'S HEAD OFF—CORROBORATIVE OF THE STATEMENT OF DANIELS.

NOTHING is here known of the writer of the following statement beyond what the article itself contains. It is interesting in connection with Daniels' narrative on account of the source from which it emanates, and it will be seen that these two eye-witnesses to the murder corroborate each other in all except a few unimportant particulars. The general thread of their statements harmonize. He says nothing about the flash of light, which Daniels testifies of, nor does he mention his attempt to cut the Prophet's head off after he had been shot, but as an admission of the latter fact would only criminate himself, it is not to be wondered at that he suppressed that part of the narrative.

Web's article seems to have been a communication addressed to the editor of some paper published in the congressional district where Thos. C. Sharp was a candidate for office, and was evidently intended to damage his prospects for election. It is stated that this correspondence was not published, but remained in the office until a change of owners was effected. The purchaser found the letter among the rejected papers, and handed it to a friend to look at, with permission to keep it over night. The borrower happened to be friendly disposed towards the "Mormon" people and allowed Elders McEwen and Wareham to take a copy of it, a transcript of which has been furnished for publication by Brother C. C. A. Christensen, as follows:

CARTHAGE, October 14, 1844.

*Mr. Editor:*

Sir—As your paper has quite a circulation in this congressional district, I hope you will find room in your paper for these lines. My reason for writing is to let the citizens of this and the adjoining Counties know who they are voting for when they are voting for Thos. Sharp, of Warsaw. I have been attending court here for several days past, and find that there are some who calculate to cast their votes for Sharp. I will now give my reasons for being against Sharp:

I came from Iowa to Warsaw, Illinois, three weeks before the murder of Joseph and Hyrum Smith. I was quite a young man, not over twenty years old, and had not much experience in life. Sharp, and some others, persuaded me to call my name Boggs, a son of Governor Boggs, of Missouri. I agreed to do so, and then Sharp circulated all kinds of mean tales about the Mormons. He often said, in my presence, that there was a "young man that Jo Smith had his father shot," which had a great influence to raise the prejudices of the people against the Mormons. He also persuaded me to join the company that was gathering there to meet the governor's troops at Carthage, which I did. The time came when we had to march to Carthage. We marched about six or eight miles and met a man with orders from the governor, that we were not wanted and to return to our homes. This word enraged Capt. Sharp, as he was called, very much. He said all might go home that wanted to; but he would go to Carthage, if he had to go alone. He said Smith ought to be killed, and if he could raise men, it should be done before night; he was in jail, and now was the time. He then asked how many of those in the company would go with him to Carthage to commit this disgraceful deed. Clerk Burs, Snar Redman and Hoakes Middleton were the first to join Sharp. He then asked if the rest were all cowards. At that, about fifty or sixty went over to him, and myself with the crowd. Jack Davis said he was no coward, but he should not go in such a company, in a thing of that kind. He and several others went back. We then organized and moved for Carthage. We moved to a point of timber, west of Carthage, and waited for Williams to return, as he had gone on to see if there were any there who would oppose us. When we came to the timber, a man came to us on a large, white horse; he brought with him a note to Sharp, stating that he would not meet with any opposition. This paper was signed by W. A. Smith, the man that had charge of the company that the governor had left at Carthage to protect the Smiths until the day of their trial.

Sharp sent this man back, to learn if the guard at the jail would oppose him. The captain of the guard sent him a note, stating that their guns were all loaded with blank cartridges, and to fear no danger. This paper was signed F. Worrell.

We then marched to the jail, overrun the guard and rushed in the jail. The door of the room was closed by the Smiths so hard that we could not enter. One of our men shot through the door and a man fell back on the floor, I supposed dead, as he never made any attempt to rise. The door flew open; I saw two men in the room. We shot at them several times; at length one of them fell on the floor; the other jumped out of the window. I ran down the stairs to see where he was. When I got to him he was trying to get up. He appeared stunned by the fall. I struck him in the face and said: "Old Jo, damn you, where are you now!" I then set him up against the well-curb and went away from him.

Hoake and some other person shot him; whether it was Sharp, or not, I never could exactly learn; but I presume it was, as his gun was empty. We then left the jail. When we got a few rods from the jail, Sharp ordered all the guns loaded that were empty and he loaded his.

I never can forget the frightened family that was in the jail. To think that a set of men would go in a house where there were two women and several little helpless children and commit the willful murder! It is too bad to think of it, and I wish I could never think of it.

Clerk said, before we got to the jail, he wished he could let the jailor know what they were going to do. Sharp said they were Jack-Mormons, and it made no difference.

I was led into this mean act by Sharp and others, at Warsaw. I can only say, I wish they had given me good advice in place of that they gave, as it has caused me to be an unhappy man ever since.

I here mention, when I went to Smith, after he fell out of the window, I dropped a pewter fife out of my hand and left it there. It belonged to a man by the name of Phelps, as I understand by some of our gang (though he was not one of our gang).

While we were in the timber, the man on the white horse brought a letter to Sharp, how to manage when he came to the jail, and spare none of them, as they were all four Mormons. This letter was signed A. Simpson. I could give the names of several more, but I will not do it at present.

I will give my true name,
Wm. Web.

N. B.—I hope you will not fail to publish these lines. I would send you the money to pay for the job; but I am a good ways from home and my means limited. I live in the south part of Missouri. W. Web.

*Testimonies:*—We certify that this is a true copy of the original.
Alex. McEwen,<br>James Wareham.

## CHAPTER X.

FORD'S FLIGHT FROM NAUVOO ON HEARING THE SIGNAL THAT THE MURDER HAD BEEN COMMITTED — PREVENTS THE NEWS FROM BEING CARRIED TO NAUVOO — HIS ADVICE TO THE PEOPLE OF CARTHAGE TO FLEE—ELDER TAYLOR'S RETURN TO NAUVOO—HIS OWN ACCOUNT OF IT—THE GOVERNOR'S ALARM—JONAS AND FELLOWS SENT BY HIM TO NAUVOO—RESOLUTIONS OF CITY COUNCIL—PEOPLE OF WARSAW REFUSE TO SUPPORT THE GOVERNOR—INSOLENT LETTER FROM FORD.

WHILE Governor Ford was delivering his unfeeling and insulting speech at Nauvoo, the cannon was fired by the mob party, midway between Carthage and Warsaw, as a signal that the deed of murder and treachery had been accomplished. The report was heard at Nauvoo, and, although not understood by the citizens, yet, from the movements of the governor and his posse, those who noticed their actions were satisfied, afterwards, that they understood what it meant. They made a precipitate retreat, and, a little way out from the city, they met George D. Grant and David Bettisworth, who had been sent with the tidings, and the governor turned them back with him, to prevent the news from reaching Nauvoo before he could get a sufficient distance away to be safe against the pursuing "Mormons."

They reached Carthage about midnight. The governor had an interview with Dr. Richards, and then went to the public square and advised all who were there to disperse, as he expected the people of Nauvoo would come and burn the town. They took his advice and decamped instanter, while he rode on as fast as he could and made no further halt until he was about fifty miles distant from Nauvoo. After a short rest he continued his hurried journey to his home. "The wicked flee when no man pursueth."

The Saints did not follow for vengeance. The tactics of man would have led to such a result; but they were marshaled under a banner whose omnipotent sovereign has declared that "vengeance is mine and I will repay." They made no demonstration of force whatever. Yet there was a general feeling of uneasiness through the country, for the people did not believe it possible that the Saints would restrain their passions.

While their enemies throughout the County were fleeing for their lives, or trembling lest retributive justice should overtake them, the Saints in Nauvoo were peacefully but sorrowfully performing the last rites over the remains of their martyred Prophet and Patriarch and taking steps to have Elder John Taylor, who still lay at Carthage terribly wounded and in a very precarious condition, brought home. The account of his return to Nauvoo is thus related by President Taylor:

"I lay from about five o'clock until the next morning without having my wounds dressed, as there was scarcely any help of any kind in Carthage, and Brother Richards was busy with the dead bodies, preparing them for removal. My wife Leonora started early the next day, having had some little trouble in getting a company or a physician to come with her; after considerable difficulty she succeeded in getting an escort, and Dr. Samuel Bennet came along with her. Soon after my father and mother came from Oquakie, near which place they had a farm at that time, and hearing of the trouble, hastened along.

"Many of the mob, came around and treated me with apparent respect, and the officers and people generally looked upon me as a hostage, and feared that my removal would be the signal for the rising of the "Mormons."

"I do not remember the time that I staid at Carthage, but I think three or four days after the murder, when Brother Marks with a carriage, Brother James Allred with a wagon, Dr. Ells, and a number of others on horseback, came for the purpose of taking me to Nauvoo. I was very weak at the time, occasioned by the loss of blood and the great discharge of my wounds, so when my wife asked me if I could talk I could barely whisper 'No.' Quite a discussion arose as to the propriety of my removal, the physicians and people of Carthage protesting that it would be my death, while my friends were anxious for my removal if possible.

"I suppose the former were actuated by the above-named desire to keep me. Colonel Jones was, I believe, sincere; he had acted as a friend all the time, and he told Mrs. Taylor she ought to persuade me not to go, for he did not believe I had strength enough to reach Nauvoo. It was finally agreed, however, that I should go; but as it was thought that I could not stand riding in a wagon or carriage, they prepared a litter for me; I was carried down stairs and put upon it. A number of men assisted to carry me, some of whom had been engaged in the mob. As soon as I got down stairs, I felt much better and strengthened, so that I could talk; I suppose the effect of the fresh air.

"When we had got near the outside of the town I remembered some woods that we had to go through, and telling a person near to call for Dr. Ells, who was riding a very good horse, I said, 'Doctor, I perceive that the people are getting fatigued with carrying me; a number of 'Mormons' live about two or three miles from here, near our route; will you ride to their settlement as quick as possible, and have them come and meet us?' He started off on a gallop immediately. My object in this was to obtain protection in case of an attack, rather than to obtain help to carry me.

"Very soon after the men from Carthage made one excuse after another, until they had all left, and I felt glad to get rid of them. I found that the tramping of those carrying me produced violent pain, and a sleigh was produced and attached to the hind end of Brother James Allred's wagon, a bed placed upon it, and I propped up on the bed. Mrs. Taylor rode with me, applying ice and ice-water to my wounds. As the sleigh was dragged over the grass on the prairie, which was quite tall, it moved very easily and gave me very little pain.

When I got within five or six miles of Nauvoo the brethren commenced to meet me from the city, and they increased in number as we drew nearer, until there was a very large company of people of all ages and both sexes, principally, however, men.

"For some time there had been almost incessant rain, so that in many low places on the prairie it was from one to three feet deep in water, and at such places the brethren whom we met took hold of the sleigh, lifted it, and carried it over the water; and when we arrived in the neighborhood of the city, where the roads were excessively muddy and bad, the brethren tore down the fences, and we passed through the fields.

"Never shall I forget the difference of feeling that I experienced between the place that I had left and the one that I had now arrived at. I had left a lot of reckless, bloodthirsty murderers, and had come to the city of the Saints, the people of the living God, friends of truth and righteousness, thousands of whom stood there with warm, true hearts, to offer their friendship and services, and to welcome my return. It is true it was a painful scene, and brought sorrowful rememberance to mind, but to me it caused a thrill of joy to find myself once more in the bosom of my friends, and to meet with the cordial welcome of true, honest hearts. What was very remarkable, I found myself very much better after my arrival at Nauvoo than I was when I started on my journey, although I had traveled eighteen miles."

The governor continued to be alarmed, so much so that he sent A. Jonas and Colonel Fellows to Nauvoo, where they arrived on the first of July—seven days after the murder. Their instructions from the executive were as follows:

"Colonel Fellows and Captain Jonas are requested to proceed by the first boat to Nauvoo, and ascertain what is the feeling, disposition, and determination of the people there, in reference to the late disturbances, ascertain whether any of them propose in any manner to avenge themselves, whether any threats have been used, and what is proposed generally to be done by them."

The City Council met and deliberated upon the matter. They passed resolutions that, for the preservation of peace, they would rigidly sustain the laws and the governor of the State, so long as he and they would sustain them in their constitutional rights. As the governor had taken from the people of Nauvoo their arms, they thought he should also take possession of all the public arms of the State. They reprobated private revenge for the murder of Joseph and Hyrum Smith, and appealed to the majesty of the law for redress, and should the law fail, they concluded to leave the matter with God.

In the remaining resolutions, the members of the City Council pledged themselves for the City of Nauvoo that no aggressions should be made by the citizens upon the people of the surrounding country, and they also expressed their willingness to "uphold the governor and the law by all honorable means while he took a course to allay excitement and restore peace, and would use his influence to stop all vexatious proceedings in law until confidence should be restored, so that the citizens of Nauvoo could go, if necessary, to Carthage, or any other place, for trial, without exposing themselves to the violence of assassins."

The same day a public meeting was held by the citizens of Nauvoo, at which Messrs. Jonas and Fellows were present, and the resolutions of the City Council were read and unanimously endorsed by the citizens.

From Nauvoo the governor's commissioners went to Carthage and Warsaw, and at the latter place Mr. Jonas made a speech to the people in which he requested them to say whether they would support Governor Ford in enforcing the law and upholding the Constitution, and they unanimously refused to give the pledge.

This refusal on the part of the people of Warsaw is in keeping with all their previous proceedings towards the people of Nauvoo, and it requires but very little discernment to discover where the wrong existed. They thirsted for further trouble and bloodshed and said that either they or the Mormons must leave the County.

The people of Carthage and Warsaw were not alone in sanctioning the cruel murder of Joseph and Hyrum Smith; the deed met with a general feeling of approval throughout the whole country, so far as bigoted priests, traitorous apostates and lawless mobocrats had been able to raise a prejudice against them. The feeling was not as outspoken everywhere else as at those places; but still there was a strong under-current of approval in the public sentiment. The majority of the people winked at the transaction, though there were some honorable exceptions. This is most clearly set forth in a letter written by Ford about this time, to the people of Nauvoo, in which he thus insults their misfortunes:

"The naked truth then is, that most well-informed persons condemn in the most unqualified manner the mode in which the Smiths were put to death; but nine out of every ten of such accompany the expression of their disapprobation by a manifestation of their pleasure that they are dead. The disapproval is most unusually cold and without feeling. It is a disapproval which appears to be called for, on their part, by decency, by a respect for the laws and a horror of mobs, but does not flow warm from the heart. The unfortunate victims of this assassination were generally and thoroughly hated throughout the country, and it is not reasonable to suppose that their death has produced any reaction in the public mind resulting in active sympathy; if you think so, you are mistaken. Most that is said on the subject is merely from the teeth out; and your people may depend on the fact, that public feeling is now, at this time, as thoroughly against them as it has ever been."

It was not enough that the Saints should have their beloved leaders murdered in cold blood! It was not sufficient that they should be sacrificed to treachery! It did not suffice that their lives should be cut short by the assassin! It was not disgraceful enough that Ford should outrage honor and humanity by breaking the plighted faith of the State! It was not sufficiently barbarous and unprincipled that he should draw his confiding victims into death's snare and then leave them defenseless, after repeatedly pledging himself for their protection! It was not cruel enough for him to thus make them the victims of a ruthless mob! No, all this did not suffice. He must send his relentless stings still deeper into the wounded heart and taunt the Saints in the depths of that grief which his own treachery had produced. After he, and his willing helpers, had shed the innocent blood, he must coolly and in this heartless manner insult the tenderest feelings of love and respect that it is possible for mortal beings to entertain for any of their race.

Ford was a weak governor. He lacked the essential qualities for a statesman. He was destitute of stability and energy. He could not brook the taunts and threats of mobocrats, but suffered himself to be moulded as their pliant tool. He descended from the dignity of a governor and walked arm in arm with those who trampled his authority under their feet.

The governor was right in what he said in the foregoing extract as to the bitter feeling of the people of the State against the "Mormon" community and their secret sanction of the murder of Joseph and Hyrum Smith.

## CHAPTER XI.

SIDNEY RIGDON'S CLAIM TO LEADERSHIP—THE SAINTS CONVINCED THAT PRESIDENT YOUNG WAS THE MAN—WORK ON THE TEMPLE CROWDED—PERSECUTIONS CONTINUED—REMOVAL TO ROCKY MOUNTAINS PREDICTED—SUGGESTION FROM GOVERNOR FORD—A SONG.

THE death of Joseph Smith left the Church for a short time apparently without a head. At the time of his death most of the Twelve Apostles were on missions in the Eastern States; but they returned home as soon as possible after receiving the sad news. Immediately after they reached Nauvoo, on Thursday, August 8, 1844, they attended a very large meeting that had been called by Sidney Rigdon, at the grove east of the Temple. After Mr. Rigdon had got through speaking, and trying to induce the people to choose him as a guardian for the Church, Brigham Young took the stand, and it was then soon made manifest to the people who was the right man to step into Joseph's shoes and be his successor to lead Israel. He said:

"There has been much said about President Rigdon being president of the Church, and leading the people, being the head, etc. Brother Rigdon has come one thousand six hundred miles to tell you what he wants to do for you. If the people want President Rigdon to lead them they may have him; but I say unto you that the quorum of the Twelve have the keys of the kingdom of God in all the world.

"The Twelve are appointed by the finger of God. Here is Brigham; have his knees ever faltered? have his lips ever quivered? Here is Heber and the rest of the Twelve, an independent body, who have the keys of the Priesthood—the

INTERIOR OF CARTHAGE JAIL AFTER THE MURDER. (*See Page 78*).

keys of the kingdom of God to deliver to all the world; this is true, so help me God. They stand next to Joseph, and are as the First Presidency of the Church."

Brother Brigham made many further remarks on that occasion which were intensely interesting and instructive, but it is regretted that they cannot be inserted here in full.

At this meeting, the Twelve Apostles were unanimously sustained as the First Presidency of the Church. Brigham Young being the President of that quorum, he became, of course, the first representative man or President over the whole people.

President Young and the Twelve pushed forward the work on the Temple as fast as possible, and took a very wise course for the promotion of peace and to restore confidence in the community generally. They published an epistle to the Church at large, which was timely and replete with good counsel, and they also used all their influence with Governor Ford and the leading men of the State to have the wrongs of the Saints redressed.

But every effort to secure peace proved futile, and Hancock County continued to be the scene of mob violence, excitement and plunder until 1846. The writer is compelled, against his inclination, to pass over many circumstances of interest; only having space to refer to some of the leading features connected with the history of the Saints during those times.

Sheriff J. B. Backenstos, not a member of the Church, was very active, and used much energy in trying to put a stop to the lawless and cruel proceedings of the mob party. One of the leading men connected with the murder of Joseph and Hyrum Smith, named Frank Worrell, was shot and killed by order of the sheriff, while he was pursuing that officer with deadly weapons, with the intention of taking his life.

It is impossible for oil and water to mix and mingle together; so was it unpleasant, at least, if not impossible, for the "Mormon" people and the mobbers of Illinois to dwell together in peace. Their religious views were antagonistic. One was truth, the other error. The Saints preached the gospel in its fullness; the other class had a form of godliness, but denied the power thereof. The former proclaimed glad tidings and universal peace to the inhabitants of the whole earth. The latter, unable to combat, with argument, the force of the doctrines taught by the Saints, were filled with envy, jealousy and malice, and the spirit of bloodshed and devastation became the predominant passion of their hearts.

The Saints had endured so much persecution from the very commencement of the work, that many of them were worn out as to their physical ability, and they longed for the Lord in mercy to point them to an asylum where they could be secluded and free from the ravages of their ruthless pursuers.

The Lord had inspired the mind of the Prophet Joseph which was filled with hopeful ideas as he contemplated the uninhabited regions of the west, where the Rocky Mountains were uplifted heavenwards as the bulwarks of liberty. He had predicted that the Saints would at some future time migrate to that region and place the trackless plains between them and their persecutors.

But how this could be brought to pass, at first the Saints could not see. They prayed for the Lord to inspire them with wisdom and open the way. Their petitions were, in due time, answered; but the path which led to such a deliverance lay through still accumulating troubles and hardships.

Had the Saints been the first to make such a proposition, it would have been opposed by their enemies. But, strange to say, in a short time suggestions were made by Governor Ford for a removal of our people to California, as follows:

"I would suggest a matter in confidence: California now offers a field for the prettiest enterprise that has been undertaken in modern times. It is but sparcely inhabited and by none but the Indian or imbecile Mexican Spaniards. I have not inquired enough to know how strong it is in men and means. But this we know, that if conquered from Mexico, that country is so physically weak and morally distracted that she could never send a force there to reconquer it. Why would it not be a pretty operation for your people to go out there, take possession of and conquer a portion of the vacant country and establish an independent government of your own, subject only to the laws of nations? You would remain there a long time before you would be disturbed by the proximity of other settlements. If you conclude to do this your design ought not to be known, or otherwise it would become the duty of the United States to prevent your emigration. But if you once cross the line of the United States' territories, you would be in no danger of being interfered with."

This letter was addressed to Brigham Young, April 8, 1845. The Saints were not displeased with this suggestion of Governor Ford, inasmuch as it was an evidence to them that he would not interpose any obstacle in the way of their removal. Yet they did not design, in case of a removal to California, to act upon his suggestion of establishing an independent government there. The Saints were American citizens, and had no desire to be otherwise than true to their allegiance. Although their countrymen had treated them with violence and proscribed them in their religious liberties, yet they could not be unfaithful to the stars and stripes which had waved over their forefathers as they fought and bled to achieve independence.

There were other influential men who suggested Vancouver and Oregon as suitable places for the Saints to colonize, remote from the scenes of their former persecutions, where they might hope to be permitted to enjoy their religion unmolested.

Agreeably with the intentions of the Saints to remove to some part of the Pacific slope, beyond the Rocky Mountains, the following song was composed by Elder John Taylor, and became very popular with the people while they remained in Nauvoo:

The Upper California. O, that's the land for me!
  It lies between the mountains and the great Pacific sea;
    The Saints can be supported there,
    And taste the sweets of liberty
In Upper California—Oh, that's the land for me.
    Oh, that's, etc.


We'll go and lift our standard, we'll go there and be free:
  We'll go to California and have our jubilee—
    A land that blooms with beauty rare,
    A land of life and liberty,
With flocks and herds abounding—Oh, that's the land for me!
    Oh, that's, etc.

We'll burst off all our fetters and break the Gentile yoke,
  For long it has beset us, but now it shall be broke:
    No more shall Jacob bow his neck;
    Henceforth he sh all be great and free
In Upper California—Oh, that's the land for me!
      Oh, that's, etc.

We'll reign, we'll rule and triumph, and God shall be our King;
  The plains, the hills and valleys shall with hosannas ring;
    Our towers and temples there shall rise
    Along the great Pacific Sea,
In Upper California—Oh, that's the land for me!
      Oh, that's, etc.

We'll ask our cousin Lemuel to join us heart and hand,
  And spread abroad our curtains throughout fair Zion's land:
    Till this is done, we'll pitch our tents
    Along the great Pacific Sea,
In Upper California—Oh, that's the land for me!
      Oh, that's, etc.

Then join with me, my brethren, and let us hasten there;
  We'll lift our glorious standard and raise our house of prayer;
    We'll call on all the nations round
    To join our standard and be free
In Upper California—Oh, that's the land for me!
      Oh, that's, etc.

## CHAPTER XII.

FURTHER OUTRAGES—MEN WHIPPED—OTHERS KIDNAPPED—FED WITH POISON AND SET UP FOR TARGETS, BUT FINALLY RELEASED—ONE-SIDED COURT—ASSASSIN RULE—OUTRAGES UNBEARABLE—REMOVAL WESTWARD COMMENCED—NAUVOO BESIEGED AND REMAINING SAINTS FORCIBLY DRIVEN OUT.

THE onslaughts made upon our people in some portions of Hancock County continued to be of frequent occurrence. The mob were filled with hatred towards the Saints and placed the torch to their dwellings and stacks of grain.

"On the 11th of July, [1846] John Hill, Archibald N. Hill, Caleb W. Lyons, James W. Huntsman, Gardiner Curtis, John Richards, Elisha Mallory and J. W. D. Phillips, who were engaged in harvesting wheat about twelve miles from Nauvoo, while working in the field, were surrounded by an armed mob, who completely hemmed them in, thereby preventing their escape, and then ransacked their wagons for their fire-arms. After taking from them every weapon they had, the mob sent to the woods for some long hickory switches. Then taking the defenceless men one at a time they forced them to assume a stooping position in a ditch, while each of them received twenty lashes across the back with the switches, wielded by one of the mob party. As there were but eight of the brethren, they were so completely in the power of these merciless creatures they could not do otherwise than submit to the torture. The mob then smashed four of their guns to pieces over a stump and returned the fragments to them, while they retained the rest of the guns and pistols. The brethren were then ordered with an oath to get into their carriages and drive for Nauvoo, and not look back, and the mob fired a parting shot at them as they did so."

Two of the mob engaged in this shameful affair were soon afterwards arrested, in retaliation for which Phineas H. Young, Brigham H. Young, Richard Ballantyne, James Standing and James Herring were pounced upon while near Pontoosuc and forcibly taken into custody by a party of the mob. They were not accused of any crime, but were informed that they would be held as hostages for the safety of McAuley and Brattle who were held under arrest by the civil authorities at Nauvoo. The guilty conscience-stricken wretches who held these brethren in their custody were constantly imagining that the friends of their prisoners were close upon their track, and accordingly "hurried them from one place to another, traveling a great deal in the night. sometimes halting for a short time, when fear would come upon them and they would again take up their hurried flight, through woods, thickets and marshes, urging their prisoners on at times by goading them with the points of their bayonets, and this too when they were almost fainting from sickness and fatigue. Once the mob were on the point of shooting their prisoners, and had even cocked and pointed their guns at them, when the alarm was sounded by one of their party that the 'Mormons' were on their trail and it would not do to make any noise, when they again took up their flight." These brethren were held in captivity twelve days. During this time poison was given to them, which failed to accomplish the fatal result that was intended. Finally the mob again determined to shoot them and their prisoners "were ordered to form in a line to be shot. At this juncture Phineas H. Young plead with the mob to spare the lives of his brethren, and offered his own life if they would only do so. The delay occasioned by this appeal saved their lives, as just then one of the mob party came riding up and reported the 'Mormons' three hundred and fifty strong coming upon them ; and again the prisoners were hurried off." Finally the brethren made an earnest appeal to the guard whose feelings were softened and they even aided them in making their escape.

Mobs filled the County of Hancock, in every neighborhood where the settlements of the Saints were in anywise isolated, and many were shot at and otherwise maltreated.

On the 25th of October, 1845, Major Warren marched to Nauvoo with a body of troops and demanded an explanation of the movements of some expressmen whom he had seen on the prairies a little way out from Nauvoo.

President Young quietly informed him why they had been sent out. It was to watch the movements of parties of the mob who were constantly harrassing and threatening our borders.

Major Warren became very angry and threatened to place the County under martial law.

Elder John Taylor, who had scarcely recovered from his wounds, in a very forcible manner, said to Major Warren:

"We lack confidence in the governor's troops under your command, and while hundreds of murderers, robbers and house-burners roam at large, unwhipped of justice, we shall take measures to protect ourselves. I, sir, have been shot all to pieces under the protection of the governor's troops. Our leading men have been murdered in Carthage, and we shall not trust ourselves unprotected again until the State gives some evidence more than it has done, of its justice and humane intentions to enforce its laws."

Judge Purple's Court, held at Carthage during the month above named, was an *ex parte* tribunal, as he would receive no evidence of a character calculated to convict mob-men for the destruction of "Mormon" property or the shedding of "Mormon" blood.

To place the Saints still more at the mercy of their enemies, the Legislature repealed the Nauvoo City charter in January, 1845, thus depriving the citizens of municipal protection.

Edmund Durfee, an inoffensive man, while assisting to extinguish a fire that the mob had set in a stack of straw, in the Green Plains precinct, was shot by the mob who were concealed near by.

The governor was petitioned to interpose his power, but failed to inaugurate any thorough measures to check these outrageous proceedings. He seemed in a great degree hardened against all such intercessions.

The Saints could not endure it. They had been patient until patience was no longer a virtue. Their feelings revolted against a conflict of force. They had had an organized armed legion, it is true, and it had the desired effect to awe the wicked and keep mobbers at bay, which was the paramount object of its creation; nevertheless, had mobbers unjustifiably precipitated their forces against it, they would have met an unpleasant reception. The fact of their giving up their arms upon the governor's order is an evidence that there was no intention on the part of the Nauvoo Legion ever to make war against or resist the legally constituted authorities of the State or nation. But the persecutions, continuing year after year, became too grievous to be borne. The land of liberty could no longer afford the Saints an asylum. The most glorious republic that ever existed did not contain patriots enough to rebuke the mobocratic element. Assassins were permitted to rule and the flag of freedom was trampled in the dust. Religious toleration had become words of mythical import in the vocabulary of the rulers of Illinois.

Where a few years before, shelter, rest and hospitality were offered to the outcasts of Missouri, now the torch, the sword, the lash and the arms of the assassin waged a war of extermination, more cruel and bloody in its results than the despotism of Boggs and the prisons and chains of Missouri mobbers could inflict. It was reserved for Illinois to consummate what Missouri failed to accomplish.

The genius of Brigham Young and the Twelve Apostles was equal to the emergency, yet the removal of such a vast number of people, among whom were very many poor, aged and infirm, was a stupendous undertaking, requiring skill and financial ability. But they set about the work in earnest and trusted in God. Companies of mechanics were organized and set to work to build wagons, make tents and wagon covers, purchase and trade for teams, etc., etc., and in the month of February, 1846, a majority of the Saints were ready for the great exodus into the wilderness.

It should be here stated that this removal was agreed upon and stipulations entered into to this effect between the Church authorities and their enemies, the understanding being that the whole of the Church should leave the State as soon as their property could be disposed of. This agreement, however, was entirely disregarded by the mob party, for the Saints were driven from the State before they had a chance to sell more than a fraction of their property, the balance being left in possession of their enemies. The main body crossed the Mississippi in the early part of February, but Brigham Young,

Willard Richards and George A. Smith did not cross the river until the 15th of the month.

The minority who were under the necessity of remaining a few months longer to try to sell their property and make an outfit, were warred against and hunted night and day, during the entire summer of that year, and on the 11th of September quite a formidable mob force began to menace the suburbs of Nauvoo. Their cannon, loaded with grape and canister, were fired at the companies of volunteers who were endeavoring to check their advance. They also fired three rounds at Esquire Wells' house, occupied by his family at the time. William Sheen and his party, who had charge of a cannon, succeeded in checking their advance somewhat, and though the mob made several attempts to outflank the volunteers they were unsuccessful.

On the morning of the 12th, Major Clifford, not a "Mormon," who had been commissioned by the governor and commander-in-chief of the Illinois militia, who was stationed in Nauvoo, notified the mob party to disperse and suspend hostilities. To this they paid no heed, but fired upon the city with increased vigor. Soon the firing on both sides became very brisk. Captain William Anderson, who displayed great bravery in the fight, was shot in the breast by a musket ball. He lived fifteen minutes, all the time encouraging his men. As he was hit, he exclaimed: "I am wounded; take my gun and shoot on." His son, Augustus L. Anderson was killed by a cannon ball. David Norris was killed by a cannon ball. Hyrum Kimball, Benjamin Whitehead, John C. Campbell and Curtis E. Bolton were wounded.

Some of the mob were killed and wounded and they were compelled to retreat.

The mob continued their firing upon the city until the 16th. In the meantime a correspondence was in progress, which resulted in a treaty between the citizens of Nauvoo and the mob party, in which it was agreed that the mob forces were to occupy the city, and the "Mormons" were to deliver up their arms and leave as soon as they could cross the river.

"Mr. Brayman, agent of the Governor of Illinois, upon hearing the treaty read, declared that it surpassed anything of the kind that he had ever read or heard of. He knew the volunteers were acting under the orders of the governor, and yet they were overpowered by the mob and forced to agree to terms of banishment to save the lives of themselves and their families. There were women and children also there, some of whose husbands and fathers were in the United States army, and had started for California on foot, over pathless deserts and mountains, to plant their country's flag in distant lands. To see their wives, children and friends driven from their homes by a bloodthirsty mob, caused Mr. Brayman to shed tears. There were others also from different parts of the Union who were eye-witnesses of these outrages, who were similarly affected at the sight."

## CHAPTER XIII.

JOSEPH SMITH ARRAIGNED ON CRIMINAL CHARGES FIFTY TIMES, AND INVARIABLY ACQUITTED—RESPECT FOR CIVIL LAW ENJOINED BY REVELATION—THE SAINTS A LOYAL PEOPLE.

IT has ever seemed strange to the writer that the enemies of Joseph Smith and the Saints in general would cling with such tenacity to the belief that they were enemies to the government and the laws of the land. Yet such was the case.

Upon this subject the authorities of the Church wrote from Nauvoo, under date of April 24, 1845, to His Excellency, President James K. Polk, of which the following is an extract:

"And here, Sir, permit us to state that General Joseph Smith, during his short life, was arraigned at the bar of his country about fifty times, charged with criminal offenses, but was acquitted every time by his country, his enemies, or rather his religious opponents, almost invariably being his judges. And we further testify that as a people, we are law abiding, peaceable, and without crime, and we challenge the world to prove the contrary; and while other less cities in Illinois have had special courts instituted to try their criminals,

## COMMANDED BY REVELATION TO RESPECT LAW. 107

we have been stripped of every source of arraigning marauders and murderers who are prowling around to destroy us, except the common magistracy.

"With these facts before you, Sir, will you write to us without delay as a father and a friend, and advise us what to do. We are members of the same great confederacy. Our fathers, yea some of us, have fought and bled for our country, and we love her Constitution dearly."

As early as August 1, 1831, a revelation was received from the Lord through the Prophet Joseph Smith (Doctrine and Covenants, page 219), in which the Saints are commanded as follows:

"Let no man break the laws of the land, for he that keepeth the laws of God hath no need to break the laws of the land: Wherefore, be subject to the powers that be, until He reigns whose right it is to reign, and subdues all enemies under His feet. Behold, the laws which ye have received from my hand are the laws of the Church, and in this light ye shall hold them forth. Behold, here is wisdom."

Again, in December 16, 1833, in a revelation received by Joseph, relative to the Saints who had been driven from Jackson County (Doctrine and Covenants, page 357), is the following commandment:

"And again I say unto you, those who have been scattered by their enemies, it is my will that they should continue to importune for redress, and redemption, by the hands of those who are placed as rulers, and are in authority over you, according to the laws and constitution of the people which I have suffered to be established, and should be maintained for the rights and protection of all flesh, according to just and holy principles, that every man may act in doctrine and principle pertaining to futurity, according to the moral agency which I have given unto them, that every man may be accountable for his own sins in the day of judgment. Therefore, it is not right that any man should be in bondage one to another. And for this purpose have I established the Constitution of this land, by the hands of wise men whom I raised up unto this very purpose, and redeemed the land by the shedding of blood."

These extracts are inserted here to show to the world what the principles of the Latter-day Saints are respecting the laws of the land. They have been in print and published far and wide for nearly a half century of time. The principles contained in them, pertaining to the Constitution and laws of this government, have been all this time adopted by this people as being among the fundamental doctrines of their religious and political faith. Our Elders have preached them all over the civilized world and our publications have defended and lauded them as being among the most glorious principles of this republic.

More than this, Joseph and Hyrum Smith, and the followers of their doctrines, have carried them out in their lives and practice. And still more, they intend doing so to the end of the conflict.

Upon these great doctrines Joseph Smith has all the time been misunderstood by his opponents. Many have been willful in their opposition, and others have not possessed the resources for correct information.

No man has ever lifted a voice on the American continent, who was more strongly imbued with all the doctrines and provisions of the Constitution than was this man, and none have ever been more universally maligned and misrepresented. He loved this as the country of his birth, and he revered the memory of those patriots who established a free and independent government upon this land.

With a fixed purpose to do the will of heaven, and with the inspirations of Jehovah upon him, he stood firm for the right in every cause, and combatted error wherever it was presented. Those who knew him best loved him, for he was high-minded, honorable and dignified.

He was a target for an unauthorized priesthood and for corrupt demagogues to aim their shafts of envy at. At last they united in a crusade for his life and made him the victim of their treachery, and now his blood and that of his brother, cry to heaven to be avenged upon their heartless and heaven-despised slayers. God will avenge that blood when the controversy is made against all those whose garments have been dyed with the blood of innocence since righteous Abel fell a sacrifice to the envy and wickedness of his brother.

## CHAPTER XIV.

### RETRIBUTIVE JUSTICE.

NO doubt all Christian people will agree with the Latter-day Saints in the belief that God is just, and that while He will reward the righteous according to their merits, He will also manifest His displeasure towards those who violate His laws.

The greatest sin that men can commit is: "The blasphemy against the Holy Ghost, which shall not be forgiven in the world, nor out of the world, is in that ye commit murder, wherein ye shed innocent blood and assent unto my death." These are the words of the Lord, given through Joseph Smith, the Prophet, and His murderers can read them and learn their doom.

If we had the history of those who have shed the blood of the prophets, it would be seen, no doubt, that they have been visited with the stings of conscience for their crimes; and evidences of the displeasure of the Almighty could be traced in their after lives. As a few testimonies are at hand with reference to the murderers of Joseph and Hyrum Smith, and other Saints who have been martyred for the gospel sake, they are here inserted.

The first testimony here given was published in the latter part of 1874, as follows:

"A lady was invited to attend a Methodist church at Peoria, Illinois, and noticing a rough box or coffin resting under the pulpit, inquired concerning it, and was informed that it enclosed the remains of the wife of ex-Governor Ford, and was supplied at the public expense. Ford was present, and he looked gaunt and miserable, and his bones appeared ready to pierce through the skin. Two weeks later, the lady attended again, and was astonished to see a similar coffin in the same place. It contained all that was left of Governor Ford, who had for some time lived, and had now died, a pauper. The lady who saw this, though she had left the "Mormon" Church, remembered hearing Elder John Taylor say in Nauvoo, that 'Governor Ford would live until the flesh would wither from his bones and he would die a pauper.'"

Also, a few days after the appearance of the above notice, the following account of the tragic fate of Governor Ford's son,

Thomas, appeared in print, and may be set down among the many cases where the sins of the fathers are visited upon the children:

"Ford's children, in consequence of his poverty, were adopted by different citizens. Thomas being taken care of by Hon. Thos. E. Moore, of Peoria. The young man served in the army, and afterwards moved to Kansas, where, with an elder brother, he followed various occupations, principally driving large herds of stock from the South.

"Last July he was going to Caldwell and stopped at a ranch for refreshment. Here he was watched by two armed men, and, after proceeding about a mile, was suddenly seized by three men before he could defend himself. They took him for one of the cattle stealers, with which the State was infested, and, in spite of his protestations, prayers and appeals for an investigation, they proceeded to hang him to the limb of a tree. He told them he was the son of ex-Governor Ford, but they laughed him to scorn and refused to examine his papers."

The following appears in the Autobiography of P. P. Pratt:

"A man named Townsend, living in Iowa, near Fort Madison, was one of the mob who assaulted and forced in the jail door. The pistol discharged by Joseph Smith wounded him in the arm, near the shoulder, and it continued to rot without healing until it was taken off, and even then it would not heal.

"About six months after he was shot, Mrs. Lawn saw his arm and dressed it. He was then gradually rotting and dying with the wound. He stayed over night with Mrs. Lawn's father, and groaned through the night without sleeping. He asked the old gentleman what he thought of Joseph Smith being a Prophet. He replied that he did not know. 'Well,' said Townsend, '*I know he was a Prophet of God!* And, oh, that I had staid at home and minded my own business, and then I would not have lost my life and been tormented with a guilty conscience, and with this dreadful wound, which *none can heal!*' He died two or three months afterwards, having literally rotted alive.

"James Head, of McComb, was also one of the murderers at the Carthage jail; he was heard by Captain Lawn and others to boast of it afterwards, and Captain Lawn drew a pistol and chased him; but he ran away. He was always gloomy and troubled from the time he helped to murder the Smiths, and frequently declared that he saw the two martyrs always before him! He had no peace.

"A colonel of the Missouri mob, who helped to drive, plunder and murder the 'Mormons,' died in the hospital at Sacramento, 1849. Beckwith had the care of him; he was eaten with worms—a large black-headed kind of maggot—which passed through him by myriads, seemingly a half pint at a time! Before he died these maggots were crawling out of his mouth and nose! He literally rotted alive! Even the flesh on his legs burst open and fell from the bones! They gathered up the rotten mass in a blanket and buried him, without awaiting a coffin!

"A Mr. ——, one of Missouri mob, died in the same hospital about the same time, and under the care of Mr. Beckwith. His face and jaw on one side literally rotted, and half of his face actually fell off! One eye rotted out, and half of his nose, mouth and jaw fell from the bones! The doctor scraped the bones, and unlocked and took out his jaw from the joint round to the center of the chin. The rot and maggots continued to eat till they ate through the large or jugular vein of his neck, and he bled to death! He, as well as Townsend, stank so previous to their death that they had to be placed in rooms by themselves, and it was almost impossible to endure their presence, and the flies could not be kept from blowing them while alive!

"Wm. T. Head, an officer in Captain Lawn's company, and tarrying in Carthage, testified that he saw a certain man raise a large knife to strike off the head of Joseph, when, all at once, and in the midst of a clear day, with no cloud in sight, 'a terrible clap of thunder rolled heavily, and forked lightning flashed in the face of the murderers, and perfectly paralyzed a number of them.

"The ruffian, who had raised his knife and had sworn with a dreadful oath to take the head off Joseph, stood perfectly paralyzed, his arm uplifted with the knife suspended in air, and could not move a limb. His comrades carried him off, and all fled in terror from the scene."

Elder Jas. H. Moyle, writing from the Southern States, in August, 1881, says:

"Bro. W. C. Burton and I met a citizen of North Carolina, named Brown, who claims to be one of the mob that committed the soul-destroying crime of shedding the innocent, unoffending blood of an anointed prophet of God. He says that he lived in Quincy, Illinois, and admits that it was a rich and productive country, but with all its charms he did not seem to have contentment, as he has been wandering from place to place ever since, as though in search of an asylum for a troubled conscience. He is now settled in one of the poorest of poor districts, where he is so situated that he can go no farther, and where he is scarcely able to earn a subsistence.

"During the extremely cold weather last winter, some of his little children were totally destitute of clothing. The neighbors, moved with compassion, collected some old clothes and necessaries of life, and sent them.

"While we should be far, far from despising the poor for their poverty, I cannot help thinking of the saying of the Psalmist: 'I have been young, and now am old: yet have I not seen the righteous forsaken, nor his seed begging bread.'

"This man has not been wandering from cruel religious persecution, but, I think, to ease a restless and discontented mind.

"In Mount Airy, Surry Co., N. C., a man named Belton was pointed out to me who claims to have taken a part in the same vile, fiendish crime, and seems to have fared a similar or worse fate, having been taken with something like the palsy. He is disabled for work of any importance, which renders him a perfect object of pity and charity.

"These are the only men I ever saw who claim to be, or bear the name of being, connected with those who slew the great latter-day Prophet and Patriarch, Joseph and Hyrum Smith.

"If these be fair examples of their kind, it certainly looks as though their sins were going before them to judgment."

Daniel Tyler, in his "History of the Mormon Battalion," in writing of San Diego, says:

"Near the foreigners' burying ground resided a miserable specimen of humanity, who stole and begged from door to door. He was one of the most forlorn of human beings. He acknowledged to having been engaged in the Haun's Mill massacre, and begged our people to forgive him. He claimed to have been one of Fremont's party, and said he had been among the Rocky Mountains for the last seven years."

The following statement is furnished by Brother Joel Parrish, of Centerville, Utah:

"In March, 1877, in company with Elder Chaales F. Middleton, I passed through Carthage, Hancock County, Ill., en route for St. Louis. We tarried there a sufficient length of time to visit the Carthage jail, where our lamented Prophet and Patriarch, Joseph and Hyrum Smith, were murdered.

"We visited a Mr. Browning, who then owned and occupied, as his family residence, the old rock building, or jail, where the prisoners referred to were confined. This building was no longer needed as a jail, a new and larger one having been built.

"Mr. Browning and lady entertained us over night, treated us very kindly, and stated that any of our Elders, passing through, would be welcome to be entertained by them.

"The room where the prisoners were murdered was, at that time, used as a parlor. We were taken therein and shown the arrangement of the room. The bullet hole in the door, made by the fatal ball that struck Hyrum Smith at the left side of the nose, had been filled with putty, but was plainly to be seen. There being a carpet on the floor, we could not see the bloodstains where the murdered Patriarch fell, but we were assured that they were still there. The stains of blood on the walls, also, were obscured, as the room had been whitewashed. The jail had been painted and kept in good repair.

"We were asked by Mr. Browning if we would like to see 'the wickedest man in Illinois,' having reference to the notorious Thos. C. Sharp, who was then publishing a paper in Carthage. We replied that we would not object to seeing him without an introduction or being under any necessity of shaking his hand. With this understanding, we went with Mr. Browning to Sharp's office. Sharp was very courteous and polite, and showed signs of wishing to shake hands, a conjunction which we carefully avoided.

"A few years previous to this time, Sharp had been a candidate for office, and, while the canvass was in progress, his opponent said, in a public speech: 'Sharp, you know if we had not sworn like h—ll for you, you would have been hung for the murder of the Smiths.'

"One of the Higbees (am not certain whether Chauncey or Francis) then resided fifteen or twenty miles east of Carthage. Mr. Browning stated that a gentleman in conversation with him asked if he ever felt any remorse of conscience for the part he took in the murder of the Smiths, to which Higbee replied: 'If you think I have not, look at my child.' The child referred to was then a young woman, grown, and, strange to behold, the entire left half of her face, on a line with the nose from the forehead to the chin, was one red mass, as if it were fresh blood, warm and dripping. The left arm and hand were also in the same condition. Higbee can see in his offspring the visible mark of God's judgment for his great sin."

Elder Henry G. Boyle says:

"While in California on a mission in the year 1855-6, and laboring on the Russian River, near where Healdsburg now stands. I often heard of an old mobocrat by the name of Kogan, or Cougan, who lived in that vicinity, and who boasted of having helped to murder Joseph and Hyrum Smith at Carthage. He often sent a request to me to visit him and proffered to tell me all about the manner of the death of our Prophet. A few months afterwards I heard that Mr. Cougan was stricken with some very singular disease. So peculiar was his case, that many people came to see him. He grew worse and worse, and lay for three months seemingly at the point of death. He suffered excruciatingly, and constantly prayed to die. He also begged his friends to put an end to his suffering, by taking his life, and even sought an opportunity to commit suicide, but was prevented by those waiting upon him. Many physicians visited him, and declared they never saw anything like his case.

"Many of the people in the neighborhood said, 'If such is the end of those who kill the prophets and mob and drive the Saints, then may we be delivered from such a fearful and terrible calamity.'"

## CHAPTER XV.

### CONCLUDING REMARKS.

THE writer has resided many years in the State of Missouri. There he has many warm personal friends, whom he believes to be too high-minded and honorable to let conflicting religious sentiments interrupt friendly relations. In that State, too, there are patriots who would honor the Constitution which guarantees to all the right to worship God according to the dictates of their own consciences. Those, also, around whose lives the tenderest ties of parental affection are entwined, have their abode there in the romantic Nodaway.

These all, it is hoped, would be willing that a people who have been so ruthlessly expelled by the mob element, should have their just rights. It is to the abandoned class, (more or less in every State), that reference has been so liberally directed when alluding to the unjust perpetrations committed upon our people.

It is very unfortunate, for the honor of Missouri, that an unprincipled partizan, like Lilburn W. Boggs, happened, in those times, to occupy the gubernatorial chair. His mobocratic proclivities stained the State escutcheon with innocent blood, and dishonored it.

With the high-minded and honorable in that State, and in all the world besides, our people hold no antagonistic controversy; but are ready to meet them as friends and members of the great brotherhood of the human race.

These people ask no special right or privilege but what they will cheerfully accord to all men, of every party, sect or creed, who are ready to act with them upon the great principles of justice and equal rights. They have never advocated a principle as being a tenet of their faith, that is antagonistic to that golden rule: "Do unto others as you would that they should do unto you." They have been ready to endure all things for the love of the gospel, which they have preached almost over the entire globe for the salvation of the honest-in-heart. They have been scoffed, derided and their names cast out as evil. Kindred and friends have turned away from them, feeling that they were disgraced, because they united themselves with the people of God. Their highest and purest motives for the redemption of fallen man have all the time been misconstrued by the wicked and ungodly, and many honest-hearted people have been blinded by the refuge of lies, so that they have never come to a knowledge of the true character of the Saints.

A greater untruth never was uttered than that the Latter-day Saints are the enemies of this or any other government on earth. On the contrary, they are friends to all, and would do good to all, if the people would let them. They have met with determined opposition from the world, but, notwithstanding this they have labored zealously and continuously for the salvation of mankind. They have felt as Paul expressed himself: "Woe is unto me if I preach not the gospel." They have received light, and they have labored to diffuse it for the benefit of their fellow-creatures everywhere. They have expected opposition and that which they have had to contend with has been in fulfillment of the prophetic words of the angel to Joseph in 1823, printed in the fore part of this volume. By reference thereto the reader will see how exactly those words of Moroni have been fulfilled, up to the present day, so far as they were to take place within that period.

It was also declared that "those who are not built upon the Rock will seek to overthrow the Church; but it will increase the more opposed, and spread farther and farther." This has literally transpired.

In 1830 the Church was organized with six members, (as already stated), surrounded by sectarian churches, many members of which resorted to violence to crush it out of existence. They banded themselves together as mobs, mainly against Joseph Smith, thinking if they could destroy him, his doctrines would cease to exist. This delusive idea followed his opponents all the time of Joseph's life. It was not so much owing to any objections they had for him as a man, a neighbor, or citizen; but his doctrines were so self-convincing and so susceptible of scriptural proof, that they were unable to controvert them; hence the ministers of the day became alarmed lest their congregations should follow after this, to them, new and strange gospel. To prevent this, they became inspired with a desire to make war upon his person, and finally this became a dominant passion with them, and some thought, no doubt, that they would be doing good service to mankind to close his career, even though it might be by the shedding of his blood. While acting thus it seems never to have occurred to them that they were bringing to pass the very things that the angel told Joseph would follow the publication of the Book of Mormon and the restoration of the gospel with the power and authority of the holy Priesthood, yet these predictions of the celestial messenger were then printed and made public.

When these persecutions came, Joseph and all who embraced the truth were prepared in mind to encounter them. They saw in them the fulfillment of the prophetic announcement, and they felt to rejoice in the day of trouble, feeling glad that they were counted worthy to suffer affliction with the people of God. They were willing to drink from the same bitter cup that was presented to the ancient saints and to the Redeemer of mankind.

Formerly, the saints were hunted and driven from city to city; they sought refuge in holes, dens and caves of the earth, and many fell as martyrs.

In thees last days, the same causes produce the same effects. Our people, with their leaders, have been hunted "as the roe upon the mountain." In the winter season at least fifteen hundred were exiled from a sovereign State, having to travel hundreds of miles with scanty clothing and with blistered and bleeding feet, and subjected to the taunts and jeers of the populace through whose neighborhoods they were compelled to pass before reaching the then friendly shores of Illinois.

## CONCLUDING REMARKS.

Our dead are strewn along the track of our exits from Ohio to Missouri, from that State to Illinois, and from there across the plains to Utah; and also mark the circuitous route of the Mormon Battalion to California, whither they marched under the stars and stripes to redeem this western region from the dominion of Mexico and bring it under the sovereignty of the American banner. And many of these might now be living had not the seeds of disease been sown in their systems by being exiled and driven from their homes.

Since the death of Joseph Smith about thirty-eight years have passed, and the doctrines he promulgated have been steadily gaining converts. Those who have embraced them have penetrated almost every country on the globe and carried the glad message to the honest-in-heart, whose ears have tingled with the welcome sound and their hearts been made to believe. Year after year has witnessed the fulfillment of prophecy, and editors, priests and people of the world, in alarm and astonishment, have repeatedly asked the question which Isaiah asked: "Who are these that fly as a cloud, and as the doves to their windows? Surely the isles shall wait for me, and the ships of Tarshish first, to bring thy sons from far." "They that erred in spirit" have "come to understanding, and they that murmured" have "learned doctrine."

The Book of Mormon has been published in many editions of the English language. It has also been translated and printed in seven or eight other languages, thus going far to bring to pass the words of Moroni, that "the knowledge which this record contains will go to every nation, and kindred, and tongue, and people under the whole heaven."

The people of the world make a great mistake when they think the perpetuity of the gospel depends upon the life of any man. Men are mortal, and must die; but truth is eternal and consequently will live forever. (Daniel ii., 44.) "And in the days of these kings shall the God of heaven set up a kingdom which shall never be destroyed: and the kingdom shall not be left to other people. but it shall break in pieces and consume all these kingdoms and it shall stand forever."

If the Church of Jesus Christ of Latter-day Saints be this kingdom, then will it stand, and the gates of hell will not prevail against it; but if it is not, then will it surely come to nought and fall.

When Joseph Smith was taken, the Lord had another man in readiness to take his place and lead His people. Brigham Young was that man, and the wonderful work that was performed during his leadership of about thirty-three years has astonished the whole civilized world. A recapitulation of what was accomplished during his presidency would be far too elaborate for the limits of this work. But the name of this champion of truth and justice is familiar to all men of reading and intelligence. The same spirit of persecution followed him that followed Joseph Smith, but he had the blessed privilege, at last, of dying in peace in his own house, surrounded by his friends, and amidst the endearments and consolations of home.

Many then entertained the idea that the success of "Mormonism," as it is called by the world, depended upon him. But after he had gone the way of all flesh, the glorious truths of the gospel still lived. John Taylor stepped into his position, with ability and experience sufficient, with the blessings and favor of heaven, to conduct the work successfully. And thus will it be *ad infinitum*, from the leadership of one to another, until the kingdom is prepared to be delivered up to the Son of Man when He shall become the king and ruler of the whole earth.

These facts are calculated to inspire hope and confidence in the midst of the Saints and should disabuse the sectarian mind of the false idea that the success of the work of the Lord depends upon the lives of men. And if it be true that "the blood of the martyrs is the seed of the church," it would be wise policy in them to change their mode of warfare against the Saints; throw down carnal weapons, and trust the success of their systems to the moral force of their principles.

What a shame in a professedly Christian country, that men should be treated with the violence and indignities that have hitherto been meted out to the Latter-day Saints! What a disgrace to free institutions, and an insult to the memories of the patriot fathers who gave their lives to establish a government that, by its laws, should protect all its citizens in the right to worship Almighty God according to the dictates of conscience! What a libel upon the professions of American statesmen, to stand still, with the stars and stripes waving above them, and they not thunder their denunciations against deeds that would crimson with blushes the faces of barbarians and savages!

Article first of the amendments to the Constitution says:

"Congress shall make no law respecting an establishment of religion, or prohibit the free exercise thereof; or abridge the freedom of speech or of the press; or the right of the people peaceably to assemble, and to petition the government for a redress of grievances."

When this amendment was made to the Constitution, it was, no doubt, the full intention of Congress and the people at large to keep its provisions inviolate. Were there existing causes for its adoption? If so, then was its creation the more imperative. And, as it still exists without repeal, its requirements are as binding now as when first adopted. Has it been a safeguard to the Methodist, Baptist, Presbyterian, Catholic, and other churches, and made them feel secure in their respective modes of worship? Doubtless it has, and it is proper that it should. But, in the practice of their opponents, the Latter-day Saints have been made an exception. They have not been protected in their religious worship. And the administrators of the law, with a few exceptions, have not enforced this fundamental law for their benefit. Why is this?

The reason is of easy solution, and was foretold by Moroni. It was revealed among the first utterances of the angel of God to Joseph Smith, when the two great powers were presented to him and the mission of each explained. The prince of darkness with his innumerable hosts began the work of antagonism the very hour the records of the Nephites were delivered to Joseph, and the opposition has grown stronger from that time in a corresponding ratio to the spread of the gospel. And as the sects are acting without authority, so far as the sanction of the heavens is concerned, they are ready to make common cause against the restored authority of the Son of Man. They have all the time charged the "Mormons" with a union of Church and State, yet what is the spectacle presented in 1882, in the United States? The various sects have united their power and influence against the people of Utah, because of their religion. They hold conventions, composed of delegates from the various sects, and pass resolutions proscribing the Latter-day

Saints in their worship of Almigthy God. And to carry their unjust aims into execution, they invite political partizans to deliberate with them and make inflammatory speeches; and they unitedly seek the aid of Congress and the President to do just what this amendment says they shall not have the right to do, namely, to "prohibit the free exercise" of religion. And, still further, if the arm of the civil law is not sufficient, they recommend that the military power of the government be brought to bear to coerce and enforce their measures, which measures aim at the complete overthrow of the political and religious rights of the people of Utah.

The Constitution further declares that:

"No bill of attainder or *ex post facto* law shall be passed."

Says one, "No such law has been passed by Congress respecting Utah." Perhaps not in the express wording; but how far short has it come of being so in spirit and in meaning? If the operations of a law will affect or have to do with conditions which already exist or have existed, how much difference is there in it and a law that is expressly *ex post facto*?

There is not space here to quote from the Edmunds bill; but every person acquainted with its provisions cannot fail to see that, if it shall be enforced according to its real meaning and wording, its practical operation must be retroactive. It expressly interferes with marital contracts already made and entered into between husband and wife in a plural relationship. It authorizes five appointed commissioners to adjudge these parties, and, without judicial investigation, and merely upon report or some incidental events connected with the case, to pass against them an order of disfranchisement excluding them from the ballot-box; and, if the parties hold office of trust or emolument, to compel them to vacate the same forthwith. A law of this kind is dictatorial and oppressive to an outrageous extent and never can be authorized by the Constitution.

And if persons suffer the loss of reputation and of civil rights generally, by an act of Congress, how much does it lack of being, in reality, a bill of attainder? And when people are attainted, not for acts of outlawry, felony or treason, but for conscience sake in matters of religion, it presents a phase of intolerance which fails to harmonize with the genius of republican institutions.

www.ingramcontent.com/pod-product-compliance
Lightning Source LLC
Chambersburg PA
CBHW031347160426
43196CB00007B/764